The Flavor Maker's Cookbook

From **Crisco OIL**

© 1984 Procter & Gamble

Design, recipe development, editing, photography and production by Cy DeCosse Incorporated, Minneapolis.
Color separations by Lehigh Electronic Color, Chicago.
Printed by Lehigh Cadillac Printing, Chicago, and Lehigh Press Lithographers, New Jersey.

Contents

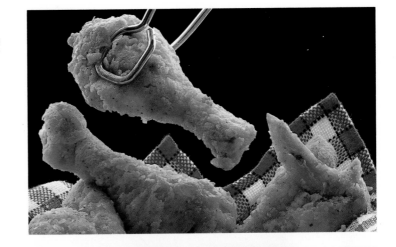

Crisco Oil...
The Flavor Maker

Since 1960 when it was first introduced, Crisco Oil's reputation for high quality and dependability has made it one of America's best selling cooking oils. To keep up with consumers' changing needs, Crisco Oil was reformulated in 1983 to blend better and improve the flavor of chicken and salad.

This special reformulation allows Crisco Oil to bond better with water and start to fry faster. This creates fried foods that are crisper and fried chicken that tastes better. Crisco Oil is better for frying than butter or margarine as it can be heated to normal cooking temperatures without spattering or burning. Whether pan-frying, sautéing, stir-frying or deep-frying, Crisco Oil gives you superb results! (In your recipes for frying, Crisco Oil can be substituted for butter, margarine or shortening.)

Crisco Oil's reformulation also allows the oil to blend better in salad dressings. The result is dressings that stay blended longer. This creates a more uniform dressing with a more balanced flavor. In 1983, taste tests were conducted with consumers who were unaware of the specific oil brands being tested. The results showed consumers significantly preferred the taste of salad dressings made with Crisco Oil to dressings made with the other leading oil brand.

Crisco Oil is also an excellent baking ingredient. The recipes in this book were specially designed to be made with Crisco Oil. Follow these recipes for cakes, cookies, bars and breads that turn out moist and delicious. Crisco Oil can also be used in your own recipes that call for "vegetable oil." However, in most baking recipes you should not substitute any oil for butter, margarine or shortening.

Crisco Oil satisfies all your cooking needs.

After 60 seconds

After 60 seconds

Blending.

Reformulated Crisco Oil now stays blended longer with vinegar. This means salad dressings have a more balanced flavor, and you get a better tasting salad with no oily or vinegary taste.

Other oils may separate quicker from vinegar. Salads tossed with this dressing can taste flat and oily or sharp and vinegary.

Frying.

Reformulated Crisco Oil now forms a bond with water when brought to a boil. In frying, this means the oil bonds with natural moisture on the surface of food, so frying starts faster. Chicken turns out extra crunchy on the outside, moist and delicious on the inside.

Baking.

You get superb results when baking cakes, cookies, breads, muffins and pie crusts with Crisco Oil. Pie crusts with oil are especially easy because there is no bother with measuring or cutting in solid shortening; you simply stir the ingredients together with a fork. The recipes for baked items in this book were especially developed using Crisco Oil — do not substitute butter, margarine or solid shortening.

Storing.

Like all other vegetable oils, Crisco Oil should be stored away from heat and direct sunlight.

Salad Tips

Serve a crisp, green salad to add nutrition to any meal. The versatile green salad can be served as a delicious entree or as a complement to any dish. Use the tips below to help make every salad fresh and attractive.

Selecting the Greens.

There are many varieties of greens available in the produce department of most supermarkets. Lettuces like iceberg, Boston, Bibb and romaine are popular because of their mild flavor. For more strong-flavored greens, try curly endive, Belgian endive, escarole or watercress. These are often used as garnishes or in combination with a milder green. Textures of greens also differ, ranging from crisp, brittle iceberg to soft, tender Bibb lettuce. When selecting greens, avoid those that are yellow, limp or oversized. These indicate age or lack of freshness. Combine two or more varieties of greens for a salad with interesting taste, texture and and color.

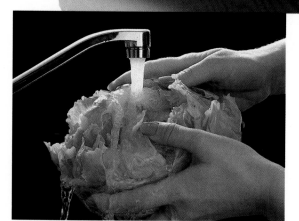

Washing and Storing the Greens.

Wash greens in cool water and thoroughly dry them before storing. Spinach leaves are usually covered with a coarse grit which needs to be carefully rinsed off. Place rinsed greens in a colander·or salad spinner, or wrap them in an absorbent towel to dry. When the greens are completely dry, place in a covered container or a large plastic food storage bag. Store in your refrigerator for up to one week.

Salad Dressing.

Salad dressings made with Crisco Oil can be prepared in advance and thoroughly chilled before using. To serve, remove dressing from the refrigerator and shake well.

Assembling the Salad.

Tear the greens with your fingers or cut them with a stainless steel knife into bite-size pieces. Combine the greens with other favorite salad ingredients like fresh mushrooms, cucumbers, carrots or tomatoes. Try apple chunks, asparagus pieces or walnut halves for something different. Turn a salad into a main dish by adding a protein source such as ham, chicken, turkey, cheese or hard-cooked eggs. Combine the salad and salad dressing just before serving. Toss with a gentle folding motion to coat each bite of salad with dressing. Finally, add a handful of croutons for extra crunch.

Garnishing.

Add color and flavor to a salad with an attractive garnish. Be sure the garnish complements the appearance of the salad without overpowering its flavor. A garnish can be as simple as a sprinkling of fresh parsley or as unique as a radish chrysanthemum or carrot twist.

Frying Tips

A quality vegetable cooking oil like Crisco Oil is the most important ingredient you need to get good taste results when frying. To ensure excellent results, foods should be prepared properly before frying. Correct utensils, heat setting and cooking techniques should be used for best results. Use the following tips to make all your fried foods taste delicious.

Preparing Foods for Frying.

Foods to be fried should be of similar size so they will cook in the same amount of time. Pat the food dry with paper towels before frying, since moisture on the surface of food causes the hot oil to bubble and spatter when food is added. As food is added to the hot oil, the temperature of the oil drops slightly. Unless you are frying meat, fish or poultry, have the food at room temperature to minimize the drop in oil temperature. Moisture on the food may also cause a greater drop in oil

temperature, making the final product turn out soggy and greasy. Do not salt foods before frying, as salt draws moisture onto the surface of food. Salt may also alter the composition of the oil, making it smoke or burn at a lower temperature.

Stir-frying.

This basic Chinese cooking method involves frying with a small amount of oil over high heat. Stir-frying is a delicious way to prepare more than just Oriental entrees. Vegetables turn out tender-crisp and full of flavor when stir-fried. Cut the food into small, uniform pieces so it cooks quickly. Heat the oil before adding the food. Stir and toss the food constantly so it cooks evenly without burning.

Deep-Frying.

This method fries foods by completely immersing them in hot oil. The temperature of the oil is very important. If the oil is not hot enough, foods will turn out soggy and grease-soaked. Foods fried in oil that is too hot will be overcooked on the outside and undercooked on the inside. Although the temperature of the oil normally drops slightly as food is added, too much food may cause the temperature to drop too much. Add a few pieces at a time, being careful not to overcrowd the food. Use long-handled tongs to turn pieces over several times during frying. Place fried food on paper towels to dry.

Sautéing.

Heat a small amount of oil in a skillet or saucepan before adding the food. Cut the food into small or thin pieces so it cooks quickly. Stir the food frequently to prevent burning.

Thermometer.

Use a frying thermometer when the temperature of the oil is important. For an accurate reading, be sure the bulb of the thermometer does not touch the bottom of the pan. Caution should be used when heating any oil, since it will burn if overheated. If burning occurs, turn off the heat and cover the pan; do not use water on hot oil.

Equipment.

Use skillets made of heavy cast aluminum or enameled cast iron for frying and sautéing. Pans with non-stick surfaces make clean-up easy. A heavy saucepan is suitable for deep-frying if you do not have a deep-fryer. Pans should be clean and dry before adding the oil.

Appetizers

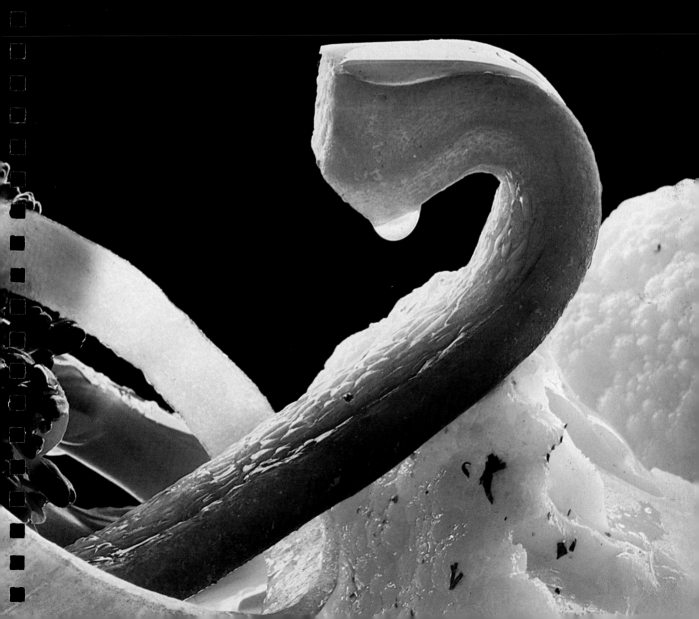

Beef Noodle Soup ▼

- 2 tablespoons Crisco Oil
- ½ pound boneless beef sirloin, cut into thin strips
- ¼ cup chopped green onion
- 1 tablespoon all-purpose flour
- 3 cans (10½ ounces each) condensed chicken broth
- 3 cups water
- 2 cups cooked vermicelli or very fine egg noodles

Heat Crisco Oil in 3-quart saucepan. Add beef. Cook over medium-high heat until beef is browned. Add onion. Cook, stirring occasionally, about 2 minutes, or until onion is tender. Stir in flour. Add chicken broth and water. Heat to boiling, stirring occasionally. Reduce heat to low. Simmer about 5 minutes. Stir in noodles. Simmer until soup is heated through. *10 to 12 servings*

Almond Soup

- 6 tablespoons Crisco Oil, divided
- ⅓ cup unblanched whole almonds, ground
- 4 slices bread, toasted, crusts removed, cut into 2 × ½-inch strips
- ½ cup sliced almonds
- 3 cans (10½ ounces each) beef consommé
- 3 cups water
- ¼ teaspoon almond extract

Combine 3 tablespoons Crisco Oil and ground almonds in small bowl. Set aside. Heat remaining 3 tablespoons Crisco Oil in medium skillet. Add toast strips and sliced almonds. Cook over moderate heat, stirring frequently, until almonds are lightly browned. Set aside.

Combine beef consommé and water in 2-quart saucepan. Heat to boiling. Stir in ground almond mixture and almond extract. Ladle into bowls. Top with toast mixture. Sprinkle with *grated Parmesan cheese*, if desired.

6 to 8 servings

Baked Artichoke Squares

3 tablespoons Crisco Oil
1 cup chopped fresh mushrooms
¼ cup thinly-sliced celery
1 clove garlic, minced
1 can (14 ounces) artichoke hearts,
    drained and chopped
⅓ cup chopped green onion
½ teaspoon dried marjoram leaves
¼ teaspoon dried oregano leaves
¼ teaspoon cayenne
1 cup shredded Cheddar cheese
    (about 4 ounces)
1 cup shredded Monterey Jack cheese
    (about 4 ounces)
2 eggs, slightly beaten

Pastry:
1½ cups all-purpose flour
 ½ teaspoon salt
 ½ cup Crisco Oil
 ¼ cup milk

Preheat oven to 350°F. Heat Crisco Oil
in medium skillet. Add mushrooms,
celery and garlic. Sauté until celery is
tender. Remove from heat. Stir in
artichoke hearts, onion, marjoram,
oregano and cayenne. Add Cheddar
cheese, Monterey Jack cheese and eggs.
Mix well. Set aside.

For pastry, combine flour and salt in
medium mixing bowl. Blend Crisco Oil
and milk in small mixing bowl. Add to
flour mixture. Stir with fork until
mixture forms a ball. Press dough in
bottom and 1½ inches up sides of
13×9-inch pan. Bake at 350°F, 10 minutes.

Spread cheese mixture on baked crust.
Bake at 350°F, about 20 minutes, or until
center is set. Cool slightly. Cut into 24
squares. Serve warm.

2 dozen appetizers

How to Assemble Baked Artichoke Squares

Press dough in bottom and 1½ inches
up sides of pan. Bake as directed.

Spread cheese mixture on baked crust.
Bake as directed.

Cut into 24 squares after cooling
slightly. Serve warm.

Flaky Ham Puffs ▼

1 recipe Mustard Sauce, page 23

Pastry:
1⅔ cups all-purpose flour
⅓ cup yellow cornmeal
¼ cup grated Parmesan cheese
¼ teaspoon salt
½ cup Crisco Oil
3 tablespoons ice water

Filling:
¾ cup ground fully-cooked ham
    (about 4 ounces)
¼ cup dairy sour cream
½ teaspoon prepared mustard
⅛ teaspoon onion powder
⅛ teaspoon pepper

Prepare Mustard Sauce as directed. Cover and refrigerate.

For pastry, combine flour, cornmeal, Parmesan cheese and salt in medium mixing bowl. Add Crisco Oil. Stir with fork until moistened. Add water. Mix well. Divide dough in half. Form each half into a ball. Place 1 ball between 2 large sheets waxed paper. Roll dough ⅛ inch thick. Remove top sheet waxed paper. Cut dough into 2-inch circles. Repeat with remaining dough.

For filling, mix all ingredients in small mixing bowl. Preheat oven to 375°F.

To assemble puffs, place one pastry circle on ungreased baking sheet. Place 1 scant teaspoon filling in center of circle. Top with another pastry circle. Press edges of circles together with fork. Repeat with remaining pastry circles and filling.

Bake puffs at 375°F, 10 to 15 minutes, or until light golden brown. Remove to wire rack. Serve hot with Mustard Sauce.

Flaky Crab Puffs: Follow recipe above, substituting crab filling for ham filling. For crab filling, mix 1 can (6 to 6½ ounces) crab meat (rinsed and drained), 2 tablespoons grated Parmesan cheese, 1 tablespoon mayonnaise or salad dressing, 1 tablespoon minced green onion and ⅛ teaspoon hot pepper sauce in small mixing bowl.

About 2½ dozen appetizers

◄ Caraway Rye Crackers

1 cup rye flour
¾ cup all-purpose flour
2 teaspoons caraway seed
1 teaspoon sugar
¾ teaspoon baking soda
½ teaspoon garlic salt
¼ teaspoon onion salt
⅓ cup Crisco Oil
4 to 5 tablespoons ice water

Preheat oven to 350°F. Mix rye flour, all-purpose flour, caraway seed, sugar, baking soda, garlic salt and onion salt in medium mixing bowl. Add Crisco Oil. Stir with fork until moistened. Sprinkle with water, 1 tablespoon at a time, stirring until mixture forms a ball.

Divide dough in half. Place one half between 2 large sheets waxed paper. Roll dough ¹⁄₁₆ inch thick. Remove top sheet waxed paper. Cut dough into 1½-inch shapes. Repeat with remaining dough. Place crackers on ungreased baking sheet. Prick each cracker 2 or 3 times with fork. Bake at 350°F, 10 to 15 minutes, or until crisp and golden brown. Remove to wire rack.

6½ to 7½ dozen crackers

◀ Sauerkraut Balls

1 tablespoon Crisco Oil
⅓ cup finely-chopped onion
2 tablespoons all-purpose flour
1 can (27 ounces) sauerkraut,
    rinsed and pressed to remove
    excess liquid
6 ounces bulk hot pork sausage
1 egg, slightly beaten
1 egg
1 tablespoon milk
½ cup seasoned fine dry bread crumbs
    Crisco Oil for frying

Heat 1 tablespoon Crisco Oil in small skillet. Add onion. Sauté over moderate heat until tender. Remove from heat. Stir in flour. Transfer mixture to medium mixing bowl. Add sauerkraut, pork sausage and 1 slightly beaten egg. Mix well. Cover and refrigerate at least 1 hour.

Mix remaining egg and milk in small bowl. Place bread crumbs in shallow dish or on large sheet of waxed paper. Shape sauerkraut mixture into 1-inch balls. Dip each ball in egg mixture. Roll in crumbs to coat.

Heat 2 to 3 inches Crisco Oil in deep-fryer or heavy saucepan to 350°F. Fry a few balls at a time 3 to 4 minutes, or until deep golden brown. Drain on paper towels. Serve hot with *Mustard Sauce*, page 23, if desired.

TIP: To make 1 day ahead, prepare and fry as directed. Cool. Cover and refrigerate. Reheat in single layer on baking sheet in 400°F oven, 8 to 10 minutes, or until hot.

About 3 dozen appetizers

Miniature Quesadillas

¼ teaspoon chili powder
¼ teaspoon ground cumin
¼ teaspoon salt
⅛ teaspoon ground oregano
1 cup shredded Cheddar cheese
  (about 4 ounces)
½ cup shredded Monterey Jack cheese
  (about 2 ounces)
  Crisco Oil for frying
  Four 6-inch flour tortillas

Combine chili powder, cumin, salt and oregano in large plastic food storage bag. Add Cheddar and Monterey Jack cheese. Shake to coat. Set aside.

Heat ½ inch Crisco Oil in medium skillet. Fry each tortilla over medium-high heat 1 minute, or until golden brown, turning over once.

Place fried tortillas on baking sheet. Sprinkle with cheese mixture. Broil 3 inches from heat 1½ to 2½ minutes, or until cheese melts. Cut each quesadilla into 4 pieces. Serve hot.

TIP: Use a pizza cutter to cut quesadillas.

6 to 8 servings

Crispy Fried Mushrooms ▲

8 ounces whole fresh mushrooms
½ cup all-purpose flour
½ teaspoon salt
¼ teaspoon dry mustard
¼ teaspoon paprika
  Dash pepper
½ cup buttermilk
  Crisco Oil for frying

Wash mushrooms and trim stems slightly. Set aside.

Mix flour, salt, mustard, paprika and pepper in large plastic food storage bag. Set aside. Place buttermilk in small bowl. Dip a few mushrooms at a time in buttermilk. Place in bag with flour mixture. Shake to coat.

Heat 2 to 3 inches Crisco Oil in deep-fryer or heavy saucepan to 375°F. Fry a few mushrooms at a time 2 to 3 minutes, or until deep golden brown, turning over several times. Drain on paper towels. Serve hot with *catsup,* if desired.

4 to 6 servings

How to Peel, Devein and Butterfly Shrimp

Loosen shell on the underside. Remove shell, leaving tail intact.

Cut down middle of back from tail to thick end, cutting almost all the way through. Loosen and remove vein with the point of the knife.

Open cut side of shrimp, flattening thick end.

Shrimp Tempura ▶

1 recipe Oriental Sauce, page 23
1 cup all-purpose flour
½ teaspoon salt
1 cup ice water
1 egg, slightly beaten
2 tablespoons Crisco Oil
   Crisco Oil for frying
1 pound medium shrimp, peeled, deveined and butterflied with tails attached

Prepare Oriental Sauce as directed. Cover and refrigerate.

Combine flour and salt in small mixing bowl. Add water, egg and 2 tablespoons Crisco Oil. Stir until smooth. Cover and refrigerate.

Heat 2 to 3 inches Crisco Oil in deep-fryer or heavy saucepan to 375°F. Dip a few shrimp at a time in batter. Fry 2 to 3 minutes, or until light golden brown, turning over once. Drain on paper towels. Serve immediately or keep warm in 175°F oven. Serve with Oriental Sauce.

Vegetable Tempura: Follow recipe above, substituting 4 cups fresh parsley sprigs, 4 medium green peppers (cut into ½-inch strips) or 1 pound carrots (cut into julienne strips) for shrimp. ▶

6 to 8 servings

Oriental Chicken Strips

1 recipe Oriental Sauce, page 23
¼ cup all-purpose flour
2 tablespoons cornstarch
½ teaspoon ground ginger
¼ cup water
1 egg
1 tablespoon soy sauce
¼ teaspoon sesame oil
2 slices bacon, cooked and
   finely crumbled
1 tablespoon minced green onion
2 whole large boneless chicken
   breasts, skin removed, cut into
   4 × ½-inch strips
   Crisco Oil for frying

Prepare Oriental Sauce as directed.
Cover and refrigerate.

Combine flour, cornstarch and ginger in
medium mixing bowl. Blend in water,
egg, soy sauce and sesame oil. Stir in
bacon and onion. Add chicken strips.
Stir to coat.

Heat ¼ inch Crisco Oil in medium
skillet. Fry a few chicken strips at a
time over medium-high heat 4 to 5
minutes, or until golden brown, turning
over once. Add additional Crisco Oil to
skillet as needed. Drain strips on paper
towels. Serve immediately or keep
warm in 175°F oven. Serve with
Oriental Sauce.

*TIP: To make 1 day ahead, prepare and fry
as directed. Cool. Cover and refrigerate.
Reheat in single layer on ungreased baking
sheet in 400°F oven 5 to
8 minutes, or until hot.*

6 to 8 servings

Antipasto ▼

2 anchovy fillets, finely chopped
½ cup Crisco Oil
2 tablespoons lemon juice
3 tomatoes, cut into wedges
8 lettuce leaves
1 jar (6 ounces) marinated artichoke
  hearts, drained
8 slices Italian salami
4 thin slices prosciutto or ham, halved
1 can (6½ to 7 ounces) tuna, drained
  and separated into chunks
8 radishes
8 ripe olives

Place anchovies in small mixing bowl. Mash with fork. Add Crisco Oil. Stir in lemon juice.

Place tomato wedges in small bowl. Add 1 or 2 tablespoons dressing. Toss and set aside. Line large serving platter with lettuce leaves. Arrange tomatoes and remaining ingredients on lettuce. Sprinkle with *capers, fresh parsley, salt* and *pepper,* if desired. Serve with remaining dressing.

8 servings

Beef Fondue

1 clove garlic, halved
   Crisco Oil for frying
1 to 1½ pounds boneless beef sirloin,
   cut into ¾-inch cubes

Rub inside of fondue pot with cut sides of garlic. Discard garlic. Heat 2 inches Crisco Oil in fondue pot to 375°F. Place pot over flame to keep warm.

Spear beef cubes on fondue forks. Fry beef in hot Crisco Oil about 1 minute for medium-rare doneness. Dip beef in *Mustard Sauce* (right) or *Oriental Sauce* (right), if desired.

8 to 10 servings

Mustard Sauce

2 tablespoons Crisco Oil
2 tablespoons all-purpose flour
2 tablespoons dry mustard
½ teaspoon salt
1 cup milk

Blend Crisco Oil, flour, mustard and salt in small saucepan. Cook over medium-high heat 1 minute. Stir in milk. Cook, stirring constantly, until sauce thickens and bubbles.

About 1 cup

Oriental Sauce

¼ cup soy sauce
¼ cup water
1 teaspoon sugar
1 teaspoon ground ginger

Blend all ingredients in small bowl. Sprinkle with *finely-chopped green onion*, if desired.

½ cup

Marinated Vegetable Medley*

1 medium bunch broccoli
  (about 1 pound)
1 medium head cauliflower
  (about 1 pound)
1 small red onion, sliced and
  separated into rings
1 large green pepper, cored, seeded
  and cut into strips

Marinade:
1 cup Crisco Oil
⅔ cup dry white wine
1 tablespoon Dijon mustard
½ to 1 teaspoon dried dill weed
1 teaspoon salt
1 teaspoon sugar
⅛ teaspoon pepper

Remove and discard tough ends of broccoli stems. Slice trimmed stems into ½-inch pieces. Separate head into flowerets. Separate cauliflower into flowerets. Combine broccoli, cauliflower, onion and green pepper in large bowl or large plastic food storage bag.

For marinade, blend all ingredients in small mixing bowl. Pour over vegetables. Toss to coat. Cover bowl or seal bag. Refrigerate 1 or 2 days, stirring or turning bag over occasionally. Remove vegetables with slotted spoon before serving.   *8 to 10 servings*

NOTE: For milder flavor and less crunchy texture, parboil broccoli and cauliflower 2 minutes and rinse in cold water before marinating.

*Pictured on pages 12-13.

Marinated Mushrooms and Onions

1 pound fresh whole mushrooms
1 small onion, thinly sliced and
  separated into rings

Marinade:
1 cup Crisco Oil
¼ cup lemon juice
¼ cup cider vinegar
1 teaspoon salt
¾ teaspoon fennel seed
½ teaspoon dried basil leaves
¼ teaspoon instant minced garlic
¼ teaspoon pepper

Combine mushrooms and onion in medium mixing bowl. Set aside.

For marinade, blend all marinade ingredients in small mixing bowl. Pour over mushrooms and onions. Cover. Refrigerate 1 or 2 days, stirring occasionally. Remove mushrooms and onions with slotted spoon before serving.

6 to 8 servings

Chili con Queso ▼

2 tablespoons Crisco Oil
¼ cup minced onion
1 can (7½ ounces) whole tomatoes, drained and finely chopped
1 can (4 ounces) chopped green chilies, undrained
¼ teaspoon salt
2 cups shredded Cheddar or Monterey Jack cheese (about 8 ounces)
⅓ cup whipping cream
Nacho chips

Heat Crisco Oil in 1-quart saucepan. Add onion. Cook over medium-high heat, stirring occasionally, until onion is tender. Add tomatoes, chilies and salt.

Stir to blend and break apart tomatoes. Heat to boiling. Reduce heat to medium-low. Cook, stirring occasionally, 15 minutes. Remove from heat. Stir in cheese and cream. Cook over low heat, stirring constantly, until cheese melts. Serve with nacho chips.

Hot Chili con Queso: Follow recipe above, substituting jalapeño peppers (drained) for green chilies.

About 1¾ cups

Salads & Dressings

Caesar Salad ▼

2 cups Homemade Croutons, page 47
1 clove garlic, halved
4 cups torn romaine lettuce
4 cups torn Bibb lettuce
8 anchovy fillets, chopped
¼ cup Crisco Oil
1 tablespoon lemon juice
¼ teaspoon pepper
1 egg
½ cup grated Parmesan cheese

Prepare Homemade Croutons as directed. Set aside.

Rub inside of large salad bowl with cut sides of garlic. Discard garlic. Toss romaine lettuce, Bibb lettuce and anchovy fillets in prepared bowl. Cover and refrigerate about 1 hour.

Blend Crisco Oil, lemon juice and pepper in small mixing bowl. Pour over lettuce mixture. Toss to coat. Break egg into salad. Mix well. Sprinkle with 2 cups Homemade Croutons and Parmesan cheese. Toss. Serve immediately.

6 to 8 servings

Tabbouleh

¾ cup bulgur, rinsed and drained
   Boiling water
2 cups seeded, chopped cucumber
1 large tomato, seeded and chopped
1 cup snipped fresh parsley
⅓ cup Crisco Oil
⅓ cup chopped green onion
2 tablespoons lemon juice
1 teaspoon dried mint leaves
2 cloves garlic, minced
½ teaspoon salt
⅛ teaspoon white pepper
⅛ teaspoon cayenne

Place bulgur in medium mixing bowl. Add enough boiling water to just cover bulgur. Let stand about 1 hour, or until bulgur is rehydrated. Drain.

Combine bulgur, cucumber, tomato and parsley in large serving bowl. Set aside. Blend remaining ingredients in small mixing bowl. Pour over bulgur mixture. Toss to coat. Cover and refrigerate at least 3 hours. Stir before serving.

10 to 12 servings

Creamy Coleslaw

⅓ cup Homemade Mayonnaise,
    page 44
4 cups shredded cabbage
⅓ cup shredded carrot
¼ cup chopped celery
1 tablespoon finely-chopped green
    onion
2 tablespoons dairy sour cream
1 teaspoon sugar
¼ teaspoon dry mustard
¼ teaspoon salt

Prepare Homemade Mayonnaise as
directed. Cover and refrigerate.

Mix cabbage, carrot, celery and onion in
medium serving bowl. Mix ⅓ cup
Homemade Mayonnaise and remaining
ingredients in small mixing bowl. Add
to cabbage mixture. Mix well. Cover
and refrigerate at least 2 hours.

4 to 6 servings

Lettuce Salad with Vinaigrette Dressing

⅓ cup Crisco Oil
¼ cup snipped fresh parsley
2 tablespoons red wine vinegar
2 teaspoons dried tarragon leaves
¼ teaspoon salt
    Dash pepper
2 medium heads Boston lettuce or 3
    medium heads Bibb lettuce, torn
    into bite-size pieces

Blend all ingredients except lettuce in
small mixing bowl. Place lettuce in salad
bowl. Pour dressing over lettuce. Toss
to coat. Serve immediately.

6 to 8 servings

Eggplant Salad ▼

⅓ cup Crisco Oil
1 tablespoon lemon juice
½ teaspoon dried oregano leaves
2 cloves garlic, minced
1 medium eggplant (about 1 pound),
    peeled and cut into ½-inch cubes
1 medium onion, thinly sliced and
    separated into rings
1 medium zucchini, halved
    lengthwise and thinly sliced
1 cup sliced fresh mushrooms
1 medium tomato, peeled, seeded and
    chopped
¼ teaspoon salt

Combine Crisco Oil, lemon juice,
oregano and garlic in large skillet. Cook
over moderate heat, stirring
occasionally, until garlic is lightly
browned. Add eggplant and onion. Stir
to coat. Cook, stirring occasionally,
about 10 minutes, or until eggplant is
tender. Remove from heat. Transfer to
medium serving bowl. Stir in zucchini,
mushrooms, tomato and salt. Cover
and refrigerate at least 8 hours or
overnight. Stir before serving. Sprinkle
with *grated Parmesan cheese*, if desired.

6 to 8 servings

Corn Relish Salad ▲

¾ cup sugar
½ cup Crisco Oil
¼ cup white vinegar
½ teaspoon celery seed
¼ teaspoon whole mustard seed
1 can (17 ounces) whole kernel corn,
    drained
1 can (16 ounces) sauerkraut, pressed
    to remove excess liquid
½ cup chopped green pepper
⅓ cup chopped onion
1 jar (2 ounces) diced pimiento,
    drained

Combine sugar, Crisco Oil, vinegar, celery seed and mustard seed in medium serving bowl. Stir until sugar dissolves. Add remaining ingredients. Mix well. Cover and refrigerate at least 8 hours or overnight. Drain and stir before serving.

6 to 8 servings

Cauliflower-Avocado Salad

4 cups water
1¼ teaspoons salt, divided
1 medium head cauliflower, rinsed
    and trimmed
⅓ cup Crisco Oil
3 tablespoons plus 2 teaspoons
    lemon juice, divided
    Dash pepper
3 medium avocados
1 small onion, quartered
    Lettuce leaves
    Radish roses
    Cucumber slices

Combine water and ½ teaspoon salt in 3-quart saucepan. Heat to boiling. Add cauliflower. Cover. Simmer until cauliflower is tender. Drain; rinse under cold water. Place cauliflower, stem up, in large mixing bowl.

Blend Crisco Oil, 3 tablespoons lemon juice, pepper and ½ teaspoon salt in small mixing bowl. Pour over cauliflower. Cover and refrigerate at least 8 hours or overnight, spooning marinade over cauliflower occasionally.

Just before serving, peel avocados and cut into small pieces. Place in blender pitcher. Add onion, remaining ¼ teaspoon salt and remaining 2 teaspoons lemon juice. Blend at medium speed until puréed.

Line serving plate with lettuce leaves. Drain cauliflower and place, stem down, in center of plate. Spread avocado mixture on cauliflower. Spear radish roses on wooden picks and arrange on cauliflower. Arrange cucumber slices around edge of plate. Cut cauliflower into wedges to serve.

6 to 8 servings

Spinach Salad with Hot Sesame Dressing

12 ounces spinach, rinsed, drained, trimmed and torn into bite-size pieces
1 cup sliced fresh mushrooms
1 cup fresh bean sprouts
½ small red onion, thinly sliced and separated into rings
¼ cup plus 2 teaspoons Crisco Oil, divided
2 teaspoons sesame seed
2 tablespoons cider vinegar
2 teaspoons sugar
1 teaspoon soy sauce
¼ teaspoon garlic salt
⅛ teaspoon pepper

Toss spinach, mushrooms, bean sprouts and onion in large salad bowl. Set aside.

Heat 2 teaspoons Crisco Oil in small skillet. Add sesame seed. Cook over moderate heat, stirring constantly, until sesame seed is golden brown. Cool slightly. Stir in remaining ¼ cup Crisco Oil and remaining ingredients. Cook over moderate heat, stirring constantly, until mixture boils. Pour over salad. Toss to coat. Serve immediately.

4 to 6 servings

Sprout-Green Bean Salad ▼

3 packages (9 ounces each) frozen French-cut green beans
½ cup Crisco Oil
¼ cup white vinegar
2 teaspoons sugar
½ teaspoon salt
¼ teaspoon pepper
1 can (16 ounces) bean sprouts, rinsed and drained
1 cup thinly-sliced celery
¾ cup chopped green onion
1 jar (2 ounces) diced pimiento, drained

Cook beans in 3-quart saucepan according to package directions. Drain and cool. Blend Crisco Oil, vinegar, sugar, salt and pepper in small mixing bowl. Set aside.

Mix green beans, bean sprouts, celery, onion and pimiento in large serving bowl. Stir dressing. Pour over bean mixture. Toss to coat. Cover and refrigerate at least 3 hours. Stir before serving. Garnish with *cherry tomatoes*, if desired.

10 to 12 servings

Watercress-Carrot Salad

2 medium bunches watercress
6 medium carrots
¾ cup Crisco Oil
¼ cup lemon juice
1 tablespoon sugar
¾ teaspoon salt
¼ teaspoon paprika
¼ teaspoon dry mustard
⅛ teaspoon pepper

Remove and discard tough ends and bruised leaves from watercress. Tear remaining watercress into bite-size pieces. Cut carrots in half lengthwise and crosswise. With a vegetable peeler, cut carrot pieces into ribbon-like strips. Combine watercress and carrots in salad bowl.

Blend remaining ingredients in small mixing bowl. Pour over vegetables. Toss to coat. Serve immediately.

6 to 8 servings

How to Prepare Carrots

Cut carrots in half lengthwise and crosswise. Shave each carrot piece into thin strips with a vegetable peeler.

Cucumber Salad

3 medium cucumbers, scored
    lengthwise with tines of fork and
    thinly sliced
¾ teaspoon salt, divided
⅓ cup chopped onion
⅓ cup cider vinegar
3 tablespoons Crisco Oil
2 tablespoons sugar
1½ teaspoons caraway seed
½ teaspoon paprika
⅛ teaspoon pepper

Place cucumbers in medium mixing bowl. Sprinkle with ¼ teaspoon salt. Let stand about 1 hour. Drain.

Blend remaining ingredients and remaining ½ teaspoon salt in small mixing bowl. Pour over cucumbers. Toss to coat. Cover and refrigerate at least 3 hours. Stir before serving.

6 to 8 servings

How to Score Cucumber

Press tines of fork firmly into skin at end of cucumber. Slowly draw fork lengthwise to opposite end. Repeat around entire cucumber, keeping score lines parallel.

Broccoli and Pasta ▲

1 package (10 ounces) frozen chopped
   broccoli
2 tablespoons Crisco Oil
2 tablespoons finely-chopped onion
1 tablespoon snipped fresh parsley
1 teaspoon anchovy paste (optional)
1 small clove garlic, minced
¼ teaspoon salt
   Dash pepper
1 cup cooked small shell macaroni
   Grated Parmesan cheese

Cook broccoli according to package
directions. Drain and set aside.

Heat Crisco Oil in medium skillet. Add
onion, parsley, anchovy paste (optional)
and garlic. Cook over moderate heat,
stirring constantly, about 3 minutes, or
until onion is tender. Stir in broccoli,
salt and pepper. Cook, stirring
occasionally, 2 to 3 minutes longer, or
until heated through. Remove from
heat. Stir in macaroni. Sprinkle with
Parmesan cheese. Serve immediately.

4 to 6 servings

Macaroni Salad

1 cup Mustard Dressing, page 46
1 package (10 ounces) frozen chopped
   asparagus, thawed and drained
1 package (7 ounces) small shell
   macaroni, cooked, rinsed and
   drained
6 ounces fully-cooked ham, cut into
   thin strips
2 tablespoons chopped pimiento
½ teaspoon salt
⅛ teaspoon cayenne

Prepare Mustard Dressing as directed.
Cover and refrigerate.

Combine remaining ingredients in
medium serving bowl. Add 1 cup
Mustard Dressing. Mix well. Cover and
refrigerate 2 to 3 hours. Stir before serving.

6 to 8 servings

Chilled Rigatoni Salad ▼

- 1 clove garlic, halved
- 1½ to 2 cups cooked rigatoni
- 1 can (14 ounces) artichoke hearts, drained and cut into bite-size pieces
- ½ cup chopped sweet red pepper or green pepper
- ½ cup cubed mozzarella cheese, ½-inch cubes
- 1 medium carrot, cut into julienne strips
- ¼ cup sliced pitted black olives
- 2 ounces salami, cut into thin strips
- ¼ cup Crisco Oil
- 2 tablespoons white wine vinegar
- 1 tablespoon olive oil
- ½ teaspoon salt
- ½ teaspoon sugar
- ½ teaspoon dry mustard
- ¼ to ½ teaspoon dried oregano leaves
- ¼ to ½ teaspoon dried basil leaves

Rub inside of medium serving bowl with cut sides of garlic. Discard garlic. Mix rigatoni, artichoke hearts, red pepper, mozzarella cheese, carrot, olives and salami in prepared bowl.

Blend remaining ingredients in small bowl. Pour over rigatoni mixture. Toss to coat. Cover and refrigerate 2 to 3 hours. Stir before serving.

4 to 6 servings

Chilled Rice Salad ▼

- 3½ cups cooked white, brown or wild rice, chilled
- ⅓ cup chopped green pepper
- ¼ cup finely-chopped almonds
- 2 tablespoons snipped fresh parsley
- 1 tablespoon sliced pimiento
- ⅓ cup Crisco Oil
- 1 tablespoon red wine vinegar
- ¼ teaspoon salt
- ¼ teaspoon pepper

Mix rice, green pepper, almonds, parsley and pimiento in medium serving bowl. Blend Crisco Oil, vinegar, salt and pepper in small mixing bowl. Pour over rice mixture. Toss to coat. Cover and refrigerate at least 2 hours. Stir before serving.   *4 to 6 servings*

Classic Potato Salad

¾ **cup Homemade Mayonnaise,**
page 44
4 **cups water**
1 **teaspoon salt, divided**
6 **medium red potatoes (about 2**
pounds)
3 **tablespoons Crisco Oil**
2 **tablespoons cider vinegar**
1 **teaspoon freeze-dried chives**
½ **teaspoon sugar**
⅛ **teaspoon pepper**
⅓ **cup chopped celery**
⅓ **cup chopped onion**
2 **hard-cooked eggs, chopped**
2 **tablespoons snipped fresh parsley**
2 **teaspoons prepared mustard**

Prepare Homemade Mayonnaise as
directed. Cover and refrigerate.

Combine water and ½ teaspoon salt in
3-quart saucepan. Heat to boiling. Add
potatoes. Cover. Simmer 30 to 40
minutes, or until tender. Drain; cool
slightly. Peel and slice potatoes. Place in
medium serving bowl.

Combine Crisco Oil, vinegar, chives,
sugar, pepper and remaining
½ teaspoon salt in small mixing bowl.
Mix until blended. Pour over potatoes.
Cover and refrigerate about 2 hours.
Add celery, onion, eggs and parsley.
Mix well. Blend ¾ cup Homemade
Mayonnaise and mustard in small
mixing bowl. Stir into potato mixture.
Cover and refrigerate at least 2 hours.

6 to 8 servings

Dilled Potato Salad

1 **cup Homemade Mayonnaise,**
page 44
4 **cups water**
1½ **teaspoons salt, divided**
6 **medium red potatoes (about 2**
pounds)
¼ **cup Crisco Oil**
¼ **cup tarragon vinegar**
1 **teaspoon sugar**
1 **clove garlic, minced**
⅓ **cup chopped green onion**
6 **radishes, thinly sliced**
½ **to 1 teaspoon dried dill weed**

Prepare Homemade Mayonnaise as
directed. Cover and refrigerate.

Combine water and ½ teaspoon salt in
3-quart saucepan. Heat to boiling. Add
potatoes. Cover. Simmer 30 to 40
minutes, or until tender. Drain; cool
slightly. Peel and cut into ½-inch cubes.
Place in medium serving bowl.

Blend Crisco Oil, vinegar, sugar, garlic
and remaining 1 teaspoon salt in small
mixing bowl. Pour over potatoes. Cover
and refrigerate about 2 hours.

Stir onion and radishes into potato
mixture. Blend 1 cup Homemade
Mayonnaise and dill weed in small
mixing bowl. Add to potato mixture.
Mix well. Cover and refrigerate at least
3 hours. Garnish with *fresh parsley,*
if desired.

4 to 6 servings

How to Fry Tortillas

Place 1 tortilla in hot Crisco Oil. Let float 5 to 10 seconds.

Press center of tortilla into Crisco Oil with a metal ladle. Tortilla will form a bowl shape around ladle. Fry until golden brown.

Drain fried tortilla, upside down, on paper towels. Cool completely before filling with salad.

Individual Taco Salads ▶

⅓ cup French Dressing, page 46
   Crisco Oil for frying
   Four to six 8-inch flour
      tortillas
1 pound ground beef
¼ cup chopped onion
1 can (15½ ounces) kidney beans,
   rinsed and drained
1½ teaspoons chili powder
1 teaspoon cumin
½ teaspoon salt
⅛ teaspoon pepper
4 to 6 cups shredded lettuce
1 cup shredded Cheddar cheese
   (about 4 ounces)

Prepare French Dressing as directed. Cover and refrigerate.

Heat 3 inches Crisco Oil in deep-fryer or heavy saucepan to 375°F. Place 1 tortilla in oil. Let float 5 to 10 seconds. Press center of tortilla into oil with metal ladle (tortilla will form a bowl shape). While pressing with metal ladle, fry 1 to 2 minutes longer, or until golden brown. Drain on paper towels. Repeat with remaining tortillas.

Combine ground beef and onion in large skillet. Brown over medium-high heat. Drain. Add beans, chili powder, cumin, salt and pepper. Cook over moderate heat, stirring constantly, 5 minutes, or until flavors are blended. Stir in ⅓ cup French Dressing.

Divide shredded lettuce equally among fried tortillas. Top with meat mixture. Sprinkle with Cheddar cheese. Serve with *dairy sour cream, chopped tomato, chopped black olives* or *taco sauce,* if desired.

4 to 6 servings

Herbed Chicken-Rice Salad ▲

2½ to 3-pound broiler-fryer
    chicken, quartered
 2 cups water
1½ teaspoons salt, divided
 ¼ cup whipping cream
 ½ cup Crisco Oil, divided
 3 tablespoons white wine vinegar
 1 egg yolk
 ¾ teaspoon dried tarragon leaves
 ¾ teaspoon dried chervil leaves
 ½ teaspoon dry mustard
 ½ teaspoon sugar
 1 large leek (about 12 ounces), thinly
    sliced
 1 cup cooked long grain rice, chilled
 ½ cup chopped celery

Combine chicken, water and 1 teaspoon salt in 3-quart saucepan. Heat to boiling. Cover tightly. Reduce heat and simmer about 1 hour, or until meat near bone is no longer pink. Remove chicken from broth, reserving broth. Remove meat from skin and bones. Discard skin and bones. Cut meat into bite-size pieces.

Pour whipping cream into small chilled mixing bowl. Beat at high speed of electric mixer until soft peaks form. Set aside. Combine 2 tablespoons Crisco Oil, vinegar, egg yolk, tarragon, chervil, mustard, sugar and remaining ½ teaspoon salt in blender pitcher. Blend at medium-high speed until smooth. While blending at medium-high speed, add remaining 6 tablespoons Crisco Oil in slow, steady stream until mixture thickens slightly. Fold into whipped cream. Cover and refrigerate.

Heat reserved chicken broth to boiling. Add leek. Cook over moderate heat about 5 minutes. Drain.

Mix chicken meat, leek, rice and celery in medium serving bowl. Add dressing. Toss to coat. Cover and refrigerate at least 3 hours. Garnish with *watercress*, if desired.

4 to 6 servings

Garden Chicken Salad

⅓ cup Homemade Mayonnaise,
　　page 44
2 to 3 cups cut-up cooked chicken
½ cup chopped zucchini
¼ cup chopped carrot
2 tablespoons chopped onion
2 tablespoons snipped fresh parsley
¼ cup dairy sour cream
½ teaspoon celery salt
⅛ teaspoon pepper
1 tablespoon Crisco Oil
¼ cup sliced almonds

Prepare Homemade Mayonnaise as directed. Cover and refrigerate.

Combine chicken, zucchini, carrot, onion and parsley in small serving bowl. Set aside. Mix ⅓ cup Homemade Mayonnaise, sour cream, celery salt and pepper in small mixing bowl. Add to chicken mixture. Mix well. Cover and refrigerate at least 2 hours.

Heat Crisco Oil in small skillet. Add almonds. Cook over moderate heat, stirring constantly, about 4 minutes, or until almonds are light golden brown. Drain on paper towels. Cool. Sprinkle on chicken salad.

Turkey Salad: Follow recipe above, substituting turkey for chicken.

4 to 6 servings

Shaved Ham Salad ▼

8 ounces shaved fully-cooked ham,
　　coarsely chopped
1½ cups coarsely-chopped fresh
　　mushrooms
¾ cup cubed mozzarella cheese,
　　¼-inch cubes
½ cup chopped pimiento-stuffed
　　olives
⅓ cup chopped green onion
1 medium tomato, seeded and
　　chopped
⅓ cup Crisco Oil
2 tablespoons red wine vinegar
¼ teaspoon pepper

Mix ham, mushrooms, mozzarella cheese, olives, onion and tomato in medium serving bowl. Blend remaining ingredients in small mixing bowl. Pour over ham mixture. Toss to coat. Serve immediately, or refrigerate and stir before serving.

6 to 8 servings

Chef's Salad

6 cups torn lettuce
6 ounces spinach, rinsed, drained, trimmed and torn into bite-size pieces
8 ounces cooked turkey, cut into thin strips
8 ounces fully-cooked ham, cut into thin strips
6 ounces Swiss cheese, cut into thin strips
1 cup broken melba cracker rounds
8 cherry tomatoes, halved
8 pitted black or green olives, halved
3 green onions, chopped

Combine all ingredients in large salad bowl or divide ingredients among individual salad bowls. Garnish with *hard-cooked egg slices,* if desired. Serve with desired dressing.

6 to 8 servings

Cheesy Tuna Salad ▼

½ cup Homemade Mayonnaise, page 44
1 can (12½ ounces) tuna, drained
1 cup thinly-sliced celery
1 cup cubed Cheddar cheese, ½-inch cubes
2 tablespoons capers
2 tablespoons chopped green onion
1 teaspoon lemon juice
½ teaspoon lemon pepper seasoning
6 tomato shells or large lettuce leaves

Prepare Homemade Mayonnaise as directed. Cover and refrigerate.

Combine tuna, celery, Cheddar cheese, capers and onion in medium mixing bowl. Blend ½ cup Homemade Mayonnaise, lemon juice and lemon pepper seasoning in small mixing bowl. Add to tuna mixture. Mix well. Serve immediately or refrigerate before serving. Serve in tomato shells or on lettuce leaves.   *6 servings*

NOTE: To make tomato shells, cut tops from tomatoes. Scoop out centers. Scallop edges, if desired.

Seafood Salad

8-ounce salmon steak
8 ounces bay or sea scallops (cut sea
  scallops into bite-size pieces)
1 package (5 ounces) corkscrew
  macaroni, cooked, rinsed and
  drained
1 cup frozen green peas, thawed
¼ cup Crisco Oil
2 tablespoons snipped fresh parsley
1 tablespoon white wine vinegar
2 teaspoons lemon juice
1 teaspoon dried basil leaves
1 clove garlic, minced
¼ teaspoon salt
⅛ teaspoon pepper

Place metal trivet in large saucepan or
Dutch oven. Add enough water to
come to top of trivet but not cover it.
Heat water to boiling. Place salmon
steak on trivet. Cover pan. Reduce heat
to moderate. Steam for 10 minutes.
Arrange scallops on top of salmon.
Steam 4 to 5 minutes longer, or until
scallops are firm and opaque, and
salmon flakes easily with fork. Remove
and discard skin and bones from
salmon. Flake remaining salmon.

Mix salmon, scallops, macaroni and
peas in medium serving bowl. Blend
remaining ingredients in small mixing
bowl. Pour over macaroni mixture. Mix
well. Cover and refrigerate 3 to 4 hours.
Stir before serving.

6 to 8 servings

Layered Argentine Salad

3 cans (3¾ ounces each) sardines
  packed in oil, drained, divided
1 can (6 ounces) pitted black olives,
  drained, divided
1 cup coarsely-broken unsalted soda
  crackers (about 16)
2 large tomatoes, peeled, seeded and
  chopped
2 medium green peppers, seeded and
  chopped
½ cup chopped onion
½ cup Crisco Oil
2 tablespoons red wine vinegar
½ teaspoon salt
½ teaspoon paprika
2 hard-cooked eggs, sliced

Coarsely flake 2 cans of sardines. Set
aside. Set 8 to 10 black olives aside.
Chop remaining olives.

Place about half the crackers in 2-quart
clear glass serving bowl. Layer with half
each: tomatoes, green peppers, onion,
flaked sardines and chopped black
olives. Sprinkle with remaining
crackers. Repeat layers. Arrange whole
sardines on top.

Mix Crisco Oil, vinegar, salt and
paprika in small mixing bowl. Pour
over salad. Cover and refrigerate 2
to 3 hours.

Top with egg slices and whole black
olives before serving.

8 to 10 servings

◀ Fruit Salad with Poppy Seed Dressing

1 pear, cored and sliced
1 apple, cored and sliced
1 banana, peeled and sliced
1 orange, peeled and sectioned
⅓ cup Crisco Oil
2 tablespoons lime juice
2 tablespoons honey
½ teaspoon soy sauce
½ teaspoon poppy seed
¼ teaspoon ground ginger
¼ teaspoon dry mustard
  Dash salt

Combine pear, apple, banana and orange in medium serving bowl. Blend remaining ingredients in small mixing bowl. Pour over fruit. Toss to coat. Serve immediately.

TIP: Toss your own combination of fresh fruits with poppy seed dressing. Create a refreshing summertime salad with seasonal fruits like grapes, strawberries, peaches and melon. Add variety to this tangy salad with any of your favorites.

4 to 6 servings

Fruited Beets ▼

1 jar (16 ounces) small whole pickled beets, drained
1 can (11 ounces) mandarin orange segments, drained
1 can (8 ounces) pineapple chunks, drained, juice reserved
¼ cup reserved pineapple juice
¼ cup Crisco Oil
1 tablespoon lime juice
2 teaspoons sugar
¼ teaspoon salt
⅛ teaspoon ground allspice
  Lettuce leaves
¼ cup chopped walnuts

Cut each beet into quarters. Combine beets, orange segments and pineapple chunks in medium mixing bowl. Blend ¼ cup reserved pineapple juice, Crisco Oil, lime juice, sugar, salt and allspice in small mixing bowl. Pour over beet mixture. Mix well. Cover and refrigerate at least 1 hour.

Drain beet mixture, discarding liquid. Line serving plate with lettuce leaves. Arrange beet mixture on lettuce. Sprinkle with walnuts.

4 to 6 servings

Homemade Mayonnaise

2 eggs
2 tablespoons lemon juice
½ teaspoon salt
½ teaspoon sugar
4 or 5 drops hot pepper sauce
1½ cups Crisco Oil

Combine eggs, lemon juice, salt, sugar and hot pepper sauce in blender pitcher. Blend at medium speed until smooth. While blending at medium-high speed, add Crisco Oil in a slow, steady stream until mixture is thick and smooth, stopping to scrape pitcher if necessary.

Electric Mixer Method: Follow recipe above, substituting 2 egg yolks for eggs. Place egg yolks in deep, narrow medium mixing bowl. Beat at high speed of electric mixer until yolks are thick and lemon colored. Add lemon juice, salt, sugar and hot pepper sauce. Beat at low speed until blended. While beating at high speed, add Crisco Oil in a slow, steady stream until mixture is thick and smooth, scraping bowl if necessary.

Cover and store in refrigerator. Stir before serving.

About 2 cups

Honey Dressing for Fruit

½ cup Crisco Oil
⅓ cup honey
3 tablespoons port wine

Combine all ingredients in blender pitcher. Blend at medium speed until smooth. Serve immediately over fruit salad or grapefruit.

Honey-Apple Dressing: Follow recipe above, substituting apple juice for wine.

About 1 cup

Parmesan Dressing*

1 egg
2 tablespoons lemon juice
¼ teaspoon garlic salt
¼ teaspoon dry mustard
¼ teaspoon pepper
½ cup Crisco Oil
¼ cup grated Parmesan cheese
2 teaspoons finely-chopped onion

Combine egg, lemon juice, garlic salt, mustard and pepper in blender pitcher. Blend at medium speed until smooth. While blending at medium-high speed, add Crisco Oil in a slow, steady stream until mixture is thick and smooth. Add Parmesan cheese and onion. Blend at medium speed until well mixed, stopping to scrape pitcher if necessary. Cover and refrigerate at least 2 hours. Stir before serving.

Cover and store in refrigerator. Stir before serving.

About 1 cup

*Pictured on pages 26-27.

Blue Cheese Dressing

1 recipe Homemade Mayonnaise,
  page 44
4 ounces blue cheese
1 package (3 ounces) cream cheese,
  softened
1 clove garlic, minced
¼ teaspoon pepper
¼ to ⅓ cup milk

Prepare Homemade Mayonnaise as
directed. Set aside. Place blue cheese
in medium mixing bowl. Crumble with
fork. Blend in cream cheese. Add
Homemade Mayonnaise, garlic and
pepper. Mix well. Blend in enough milk
to make desired consistency.

Cover and store in refrigerator. Stir
before serving.

About 2 cups

Vinaigrette Dressing

¾ cup Crisco Oil
⅓ cup red wine vinegar
1 tablespoon snipped fresh parsley
1 teaspoon Worcestershire sauce
½ teaspoon salt
¼ teaspoon dry mustard
¼ teaspoon pepper
1 clove garlic, minced

Combine all ingredients in jar. Cover
tightly and shake until blended.

Store covered in
refrigerator.
Shake before
serving.

About 1 cup

Mustard Dressing

3 egg yolks
2 tablespoons prepared yellow or
  brown mustard
1 tablespoon lemon juice
2 teaspoons cider vinegar
2 teaspoons sugar
¾ teaspoon seasoned salt
3 or 4 drops hot pepper sauce
1½ cups Crisco Oil

Place egg yolks in medium mixing
bowl. Beat at high speed of electric
mixer until thick and lemon colored.
Add mustard, lemon juice, vinegar,
sugar, seasoned salt and hot pepper
sauce. Beat at low speed until blended.
While beating at medium-high speed,
add Crisco Oil in a slow, steady stream
until mixture thickens, scraping bowl
if necessary.

Cover and store in refrigerator. Stir
before serving.

About 2 cups

French Dressing

⅔ cup Crisco Oil
½ cup catsup
2 tablespoons white wine vinegar
1 tablespoon sugar
1 teaspoon paprika
½ teaspoon dry mustard

Combine all ingredients in blender
pitcher. Blend at medium to high speed
until smooth (at least 2 minutes),
stopping to scrape pitcher
if necessary.

Cover and store in refrigerator. Stir
before serving.

About 1¼ cups

Garlic Dressing

7 cloves garlic, divided
¾ cup Crisco Oil, divided
3 tablespoons white wine vinegar
½ teaspoon salt
½ teaspoon freeze-dried chives
¼ teaspoon dry mustard
⅛ teaspoon pepper

Cut 6 garlic cloves in half. Mince
remaining clove and set aside.

Heat ¼ cup Crisco Oil in small skillet.
Add halved garlic cloves. Cook over
low heat, stirring occasionally, about 5
minutes, or until garlic is golden brown.
Remove from heat. Cool. Remove and
discard garlic.

Transfer garlic-flavored oil to jar. Add
remaining ingredients, remaining ½ cup
Crisco Oil and minced garlic. Cover
tightly and shake until blended.
Refrigerate at least 2 hours. Shake
before serving.

Store covered in refrigerator. Shake
before serving.

About 1 cup

◄Homemade Croutons

6 cups cubed stale bread, ½ to 1-inch cubes (7 or 8 slices bread)
⅔ cup Crisco Oil
½ teaspoon garlic powder
½ teaspoon paprika
¼ teaspoon salt

Preheat oven to 300°F. Place bread cubes in medium mixing bowl. Blend Crisco Oil, garlic powder, paprika and salt in small mixing bowl. Pour over bread cubes. Toss to coat. Spread cubes on 15 × 10-inch jelly roll pan. Bake at 300°F, 50 to 60 minutes, or until golden brown and crisp, stirring after half the time. Cool completely. Sprinkle on salads or casseroles.

Herbed Croutons: Follow recipe above, except place ⅓ cup of the Crisco Oil in small skillet. Substitute onion powder for garlic powder. Add onion powder, paprika and salt to Crisco Oil in small skillet. Add 1 teaspoon dried basil leaves and ½ teaspoon dried oregano leaves. Cook over moderate heat, stirring occasionally, 2 to 3 minutes. Remove from heat. Stir in remaining ⅓ cup Crisco Oil. Pour over bread cubes. Toss to coat. Continue as directed.

Parmesan Croutons: Follow recipe for Homemade Croutons above, except place baked, slightly-cooled croutons in large plastic food storage bag. Add ¼ cup grated Parmesan cheese. Shake to coat croutons. Remove from bag. Spread on baking pan to cool completely.

4 cups

Meats &
Main Dishes

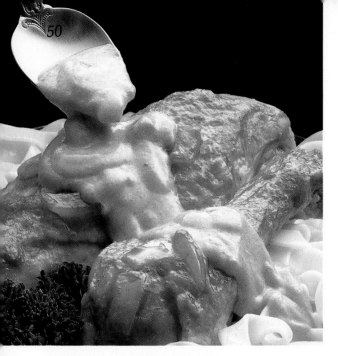

Fried Chicken*

⅓ cup all-purpose flour
½ teaspoon salt
½ teaspoon paprika
¼ teaspoon garlic powder
¼ teaspoon pepper
1 can (5.3 ounces) evaporated milk
2½ to 3-pound broiler-fryer chicken,
   cut up
¼ cup Crisco Oil

Mix flour, salt, paprika, garlic powder and pepper in large plastic food storage bag. Set aside. Pour evaporated milk into bowl. Dip chicken in evaporated milk. Add a few chicken pieces to food storage bag. Shake to coat. Remove chicken from bag. Repeat with remaining chicken.

Heat Crisco Oil in large skillet. Add chicken. Brown over medium-high heat. Cook over moderate heat about 25 minutes, or until meat near bone is no longer pink and juices run clear, turning pieces over frequently.

4 servings

Pictured on pages 48-49.

◄ Chicken Paprika

2½ to 3-pound broiler-fryer chicken,
   cut up
1 teaspoon salt, divided
¼ teaspoon pepper, divided
¼ cup Crisco Oil
1 medium onion, chopped
1 can (8 ounces) tomato sauce
½ cup water, divided
1½ to 2 tablespoons paprika
1 cup dairy sour cream
¼ cup all-purpose flour
   Hot cooked narrow egg noodles

Sprinkle chicken with ½ teaspoon salt and ⅛ teaspoon pepper. Heat Crisco Oil in large skillet. Add chicken pieces. Brown over medium-high heat. Remove chicken from skillet; set aside. Discard drippings, reserving 1 tablespoon in skillet. Add onion. Sauté over moderate heat until tender. Stir in tomato sauce, ¼ cup water, paprika, remaining ½ teaspoon salt and remaining ⅛ teaspoon pepper. Add chicken. Heat to boiling. Cover. Reduce heat. Simmer, stirring occasionally, 35 to 40 minutes, or until chicken is tender and meat near bone is no longer pink. Remove chicken from skillet; set aside.

Blend sour cream, remaining ¼ cup water and flour in small mixing bowl. Blend into mixture in skillet. Cook over low heat, stirring constantly, until thickened. Serve with chicken and egg noodles. Garnish with *fresh parsley sprigs,* if desired.

4 servings

Curried Chicken

- 1 **medium onion, halved**
- 2 **tablespoons Crisco Oil**
- 1 **to 2 tablespoons curry powder**
- 2½ **to 3-pound broiler-fryer chicken, cut up**
- 1 **can (16 ounces) whole tomatoes, undrained, cut up**
- 2 **medium white potatoes, peeled and cut into eighths**
- 1 **teaspoon salt**
- 3 **to 4 cups water**
- 2 **cans (15 ounces each) butter beans, drained**
- 1 **tablespoon lemon juice**

Cut one onion half into 4 pieces. Set aside. Chop remaining half. Heat Crisco Oil in Dutch oven. Add chopped onion. Sauté over moderate heat until tender. Stir in curry powder. Cook, stirring constantly, 1 minute. Add chicken. Stir to coat with curry mixture. Stir in tomatoes, potatoes, salt and remaining onion. Add enough water to just cover mixture. Heat to boiling. Cover. Reduce heat. Simmer, stirring occasionally, 1 to 1¼ hours, or until chicken is tender and meat near bone is no longer pink.

Remove ½ cup cooking liquid and place in blender pitcher. Add 1 can butter beans. Blend until smooth. Add blended mixture, lemon juice and remaining 1 can butter beans to chicken. Mix well. Serve with *hot cooked rice*, if desired.

4 servings

Grilled Deviled Chicken ▼

- ¼ **cup catsup**
- ¼ **cup Crisco Oil**
- 2 **tablespoons lemon juice**
- 1 **tablespoon chili powder**
- 1 **teaspoon lemon pepper seasoning**
- ½ **teaspoon ground oregano**
- ½ **teaspoon onion powder**
- ⅛ **teaspoon cayenne**
- 2½ **to 3-pound broiler-fryer chicken, cut up**

Combine all ingredients except chicken in small bowl. Mix well. Set aside.

Place chicken on seasoned cooking grids over medium coals. Grill, turning over frequently, 45 to 60 minutes, or until juices run clear and meat near bone is no longer pink. Brush with sauce during last 15 minutes.

4 servings

Spiced Chicken with Fruit Sauce

⅓ cup all-purpose flour
¾ teaspoon salt
1¼ teaspoons ground allspice, divided
½ teaspoon paprika
¼ teaspoon ground ginger
¼ teaspoon cayenne
⅛ teaspoon garlic powder
2½ to 3-pound broiler-fryer chicken, cut up
6 tablespoons Crisco Oil, divided
1 small onion, halved and thinly sliced
1 can (16 ounces) dark sweet cherries
1 tablespoon lemon juice
1 tablespoon cornstarch
2 teaspoons sugar
1 teaspoon instant chicken bouillon granules
1 can (11 ounces) mandarin orange sections, drained
1 can (8 ounces) apricot halves, drained

Preheat oven to 350°F. Mix flour, salt, ½ teaspoon allspice, paprika, ginger, cayenne and garlic powder in large plastic food storage bag. Add a few chicken pieces. Shake to coat. Remove chicken from bag. Repeat with remaining chicken.

Heat 4 tablespoons Crisco Oil in large skillet. Add chicken. Brown over medium-high heat. Transfer chicken to 13 × 9-inch baking dish. Cover dish with aluminum foil. Bake at 350°F, about 30 minutes. Remove aluminum foil. Bake 10 to 20 minutes longer, or until juices run clear and meat near bone is no longer pink.

Meanwhile, heat remaining 2 tablespoons Crisco Oil in medium saucepan. Add onion. Sauté over moderate heat until tender. Remove from heat. Drain cherries, reserving juice. Set cherries aside. Add reserved cherry juice, lemon juice, cornstarch, sugar, bouillon granules and remaining ¾ teaspoon allspice to onion in saucepan. Heat to boiling, stirring constantly.

Boil 1 minute, or until thickened, stirring constantly. Stir in cherries, orange sections and apricot halves. Remove from heat. Serve over baked chicken.   *4 servings*

Chicken Cacciatore ▼

- ⅓ cup all-purpose flour
- 2½ to 3-pound broiler-fryer chicken, cut up
- ¼ cup Crisco Oil
- 1 medium onion, thinly sliced and separated into rings
- ½ cup chopped green pepper
- 2 cloves garlic, minced
- 1 can (16 ounces) whole tomatoes, undrained
- 1 can (8 ounces) tomato sauce
- 1 can (4 ounces) sliced mushrooms, drained
- ¾ teaspoon salt
- ½ teaspoon dried oregano leaves
  Hot cooked noodles

Place flour in large plastic food storage bag. Add a few chicken pieces. Shake to coat. Remove chicken from bag. Repeat with remaining chicken. Heat Crisco Oil in large skillet. Add chicken. Brown over medium-high heat. Remove chicken from skillet; set aside. Add onion, green pepper and garlic to skillet. Sauté over moderate heat until tender. Add tomatoes, tomato sauce, mushrooms, salt and oregano, stirring to break apart tomatoes. Place chicken pieces on top of tomato mixture. Cover. Reduce heat. Simmer 30 to 40 minutes, or until chicken is tender and meat near bone is no longer pink. Serve with noodles.

4 servings

Herb Roasted Chicken

- 2½ to 3-pound broiler-fryer chicken
- 2 cloves garlic, quartered
- ¼ cup Crisco Oil
- 1 tablespoon lime juice
- 1 teaspoon dried tarragon leaves
- 1 teaspoon dried chervil leaves
- ½ teaspoon dried thyme leaves
  Pepper

Preheat oven to 375°F. Lift skin from chicken breast and place 6 pieces garlic between skin and meat. Cut slit in each drumstick. Insert a piece of garlic into each slit.

Blend Crisco Oil and lime juice in small bowl. Brush on chicken. Mix tarragon, chervil and thyme in another small bowl. Rub onto chicken. Sprinkle chicken with pepper.

Place chicken, breast-side up, in roasting pan. Bake at 375°F, 1¼ to 1½ hours, or until juices run clear and meat near bone is no longer pink, brushing with lime juice mixture several times. Let stand 10 minutes before carving.

4 servings

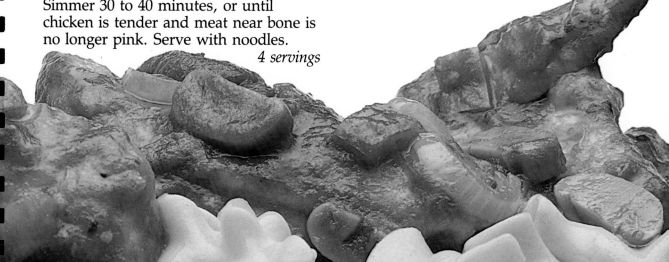

Moo Goo Gai Pan

2 tablespoons cornstarch
2 tablespoons water
3 whole boneless chicken breasts,
    skinned, cut into 1-inch pieces
½ teaspoon salt
⅛ teaspoon pepper
¼ cup Crisco Oil
¼ cup chopped green onions
2 cups sliced fresh mushrooms
1 jar (2 ounces) sliced pimiento,
    drained
1 teaspoon ground ginger
1 can (14½ ounces) chicken broth
2 packages (6 to 7 ounces each)
    frozen pea pods
    Hot cooked rice

Blend cornstarch and water in small
bowl until smooth. Set aside.

Sprinkle chicken with salt and pepper.
Heat Crisco Oil in large skillet or wok.
Add chicken. Stir-fry over medium-high
heat until no longer pink. Remove
chicken from skillet. Add onion to
skillet. Stir-fry over medium-high heat
1 minute. Stir in mushrooms, pimiento
and ginger. Cook, stirring constantly,
2 to 3 minutes, or until mushrooms are
tender. Add chicken broth and pea
pods. Heat to boiling, stirring to break
apart pea pods. Add cornstarch
mixture. Heat to boiling, stirring
constantly. Boil 1 minute. Remove from
heat. Stir in chicken. Serve with rice.
Sprinkle with *toasted almonds* and serve
with *soy sauce*, if desired.

6 to 8 servings

Chicken Walnut Stir-Fry

5 tablespoons Crisco Oil, divided
5 teaspoons soy sauce, divided
3 teaspoons cornstarch, divided
2 whole boneless chicken breasts,
    skinned, cut into 1-inch pieces
½ cup chicken broth
½ teaspoon ground ginger
½ teaspoon dried crushed red pepper
1 medium onion, cut into 1-inch
    pieces
1 clove garlic, minced
½ pound fresh broccoli, cut into 1-inch
    pieces
½ cup coarsely-chopped walnuts
    Hot cooked rice

Mix 1 tablespoon Crisco Oil,
2 teaspoons soy sauce and 1 teaspoon
cornstarch in small mixing bowl. Add
chicken. Stir to coat. Cover and
refrigerate about 30 minutes.

Mix chicken broth, ginger, remaining
3 teaspoons soy sauce and remaining
2 teaspoons cornstarch in small bowl.
Set aside.

Heat remaining 4 tablespoons Crisco Oil
in large skillet. Add refrigerated chicken
mixture and red pepper. Stir-fry over
medium-high heat until chicken is no
longer pink. Remove chicken from
skillet; set aside. Add onion and garlic
to skillet. Stir-fry over medium-high
heat until onion is tender. Add broccoli.
Stir-fry until tender. Add chicken and
chicken broth mixture. Cook, stirring
constantly, until thickened. Stir in
walnuts. Serve with rice.

4 servings

Left to right: Moo Goo Gai Pan, Chicken Walnut Stir-Fry, Sweet-and-Sour Chicken

Sweet-and-Sour Chicken

1 can (16 ounces) whole tomatoes
½ cup plum jelly
¼ cup cider vinegar
1 tablespoon sugar
1 tablespoon cornstarch
1 tablespoon soy sauce
1 teaspoon instant chicken bouillon
  granules

Batter:
½ cup water
⅓ cup all-purpose flour
⅓ cup cornstarch
1 teaspoon salt
⅛ teaspoon garlic powder
⅛ teaspoon pepper

1 whole boneless chicken breast,
  skinned, cut into 1 to 1½-inch
  pieces
1 large green pepper, cored, seeded
  and cut into 1-inch pieces
4 green onions, cut into 1-inch pieces
1 can (8 ounces) pineapple chunks,
  drained
  Crisco Oil for frying
  Hot cooked rice

Drain tomatoes, reserving ¼ cup juice. Cut up tomatoes and set aside. Blend reserved juice, plum jelly, vinegar, sugar, cornstarch, soy sauce and bouillon granules in small mixing bowl. Set aside.

For batter, blend all ingredients in small mixing bowl. Add chicken. Stir to coat. Heat 2 to 3 inches Crisco Oil in large saucepan to 350°F. Remove several pieces chicken from batter with slotted spoon. Add to Crisco Oil. Fry 3 to 4 minutes, or until light golden brown. Drain on paper towels. Repeat with remaining chicken.

Discard Crisco Oil, reserving 2 tablespoons in saucepan. Add green pepper and onion. Stir-fry over medium-high heat about 3 minutes, or until tender. Stir in tomato juice mixture. Heat to boiling, stirring constantly. Continue to boil 1 minute, stirring constantly. Stir in pineapple chunks, chicken and tomatoes. Cook 1 to 2 minutes longer. Serve with rice.

4 servings

Chicken Livers in Wine Sauce

¼ cup Crisco Oil
1 medium onion, cut into 8 pieces
½ cup chopped celery
¼ cup snipped fresh parsley
1 clove garlic, minced
⅓ cup all-purpose flour
¾ teaspoon salt
¼ teaspoon pepper
1 pound chicken livers, drained
½ cup water
½ cup milk
3 tablespoons white wine
¾ teaspoon instant chicken bouillon
    granules
½ teaspoon dried rosemary leaves
    Hot cooked egg noodles

Heat Crisco Oil in large skillet. Add onion, celery, parsley and garlic. Sauté over moderate heat until onion is tender. Set aside.

Mix flour, salt and pepper in large plastic food storage bag. Add livers. Shake to coat. Add livers and any remaining flour mixture to onion mixture. Brown livers over medium-high heat, stirring occasionally. Stir in water, milk, wine, bouillon granules and rosemary. Heat to boiling, stirring constantly. Cover. Reduce heat. Simmer, stirring occasionally, 7 to 10 minutes, or until livers are no longer pink. Serve with noodles.

4 to 6 servings

◀ Chicken Breasts with Artichoke Cheese Stuffing

¼ cup **Homemade Mayonnaise,**
   page 44
4 **whole boneless chicken breasts,**
   skinned and halved lengthwise
1½ cups **shredded Monterey Jack**
   cheese (about 6 ounces)
1 tablespoon **finely-chopped onion**
1 tablespoon **dried parsley flakes**
1 teaspoon **Dijon mustard**
1 jar (6 ounces) **marinated artichoke**
   hearts, drained
⅓ cup **all-purpose flour**
¼ teaspoon **salt**
⅛ teaspoon **pepper**
1 **egg**
2 tablespoons **water**
1 cup **seasoned dry bread crumbs**
⅓ cup **Crisco Oil**

Prepare Homemade Mayonnaise as
directed. Cover and refrigerate.

Pound chicken breasts to ¼-inch
thickness. Set aside. Mix cheese, ¼ cup
Homemade Mayonnaise, onion, parsley
flakes and mustard in small mixing
bowl. Cut artichoke hearts into bite-size
pieces. Stir into cheese mixture. Spread
about ¼ cup cheese mixture in center of
each piece of chicken. Roll up and
secure edges with wooden picks. Mix
flour, salt and pepper in shallow dish.
Dip rolled chicken in flour mixture to
coat. Set aside.

Mix egg and water in shallow dish.
Place bread crumbs in another shallow
dish or on sheet of waxed paper. Dip
rolled chicken in egg mixture, then in
bread crumbs, pressing to coat
thoroughly. Cover and refrigerate
coated chicken about 1 hour.

Preheat oven to 350°F. Place Crisco Oil
in 13 × 9-inch baking pan. Place in oven

10 minutes. Remove from oven. Use
tongs to roll coated chicken in hot
Crisco Oil. Arrange chicken in pan.
Bake at 350°F, 35 minutes, or until
golden brown.

8 servings

How to Stuff Chicken Breasts

Spread filling down center of each
chicken piece, leaving a ½-inch border.

Roll up chicken piece, starting with
shorter end.

Secure end with wooden picks.

Chicken Breasts in Wine Sauce ▲

⅓ cup plus 2 tablespoons all-purpose
    flour, divided
½ teaspoon onion salt
¼ teaspoon pepper
 2 whole chicken breasts, skinned and
    halved lengthwise
 3 tablespoons Crisco Oil
 2 small onions, cut into thirds
⅔ cup white wine
 1 teaspoon instant chicken bouillon
    granules
½ teaspoon dried tarragon leaves
¾ cup half-and-half

Mix ⅓ cup flour, onion salt and pepper
in large plastic food storage bag. Add
chicken. Shake to coat.

Heat Crisco Oil in large skillet. Add
chicken. Brown over medium-high heat.
Add onion, wine, bouillon granules and
tarragon. Heat to boiling. Cover. Reduce
heat. Simmer about 20 minutes, or until
juices run clear and meat near bone is
no longer pink. Transfer chicken to
serving platter. Cover to keep warm.
Remove and discard onion.

Place half-and-half in small bowl. Blend
in remaining 2 tablespoons flour. Stir
into drippings in large skillet. Cook
over medium-low heat, stirring
constantly, until thickened and bubbly.
Serve with chicken.

4 servings

Chicken and Vegetable Pie ▼

3⅓ cups water, divided
1½ cups cubed potatoes, ½-inch cubes
 ¾ teaspoon salt
 3 tablespoons Crisco Oil
 1 small onion, thinly sliced
 2 tablespoons plus 1 teaspoon
  all-purpose flour
 1 tablespoon instant chicken bouillon
  granules
 1 teaspoon dried parsley flakes
 ¼ to ½ teaspoon dried thyme leaves
 ¼ teaspoon pepper
 1 cup milk
1½ cups cut-up cooked chicken or
  turkey
 ½ cup frozen corn
 ½ cup frozen green peas
 1 can (4 ounces) mushroom stems
  and pieces, drained
 1 recipe Pastry for Two Crust Pie,
  page 114

Combine 3 cups water, potatoes and
salt in 2-quart saucepan. Heat to
boiling. Cover. Reduce heat.
Simmer about 10 minutes, or
until potatoes are tender.
Drain. Set aside.

Heat Crisco Oil in
medium saucepan. Add
onion. Sauté over
moderate heat until

tender. Stir in flour, bouillon granules,
parsley flakes, thyme and pepper. Blend
in milk and remaining ⅓ cup water.
Cook over moderate heat, stirring
constantly, until thickened and bubbly.
Remove from heat. Add potatoes,
chicken, corn, peas and mushrooms.
Stir to break apart corn and peas.
Set aside.

Preheat oven to 425°F. Prepare dough
for Pastry for Two Crust Pie. Roll and fit
into 9-inch pie plate as directed. Fill
with chicken mixture. Top with
remaining pastry; flute edges. Cut slits
in top. Place in oven. Immediately
reduce temperature to 325°F. Bake
at 325°F, 45 to 60 minutes, or
until filling is hot and crust
is flaky.

4 to 6 servings

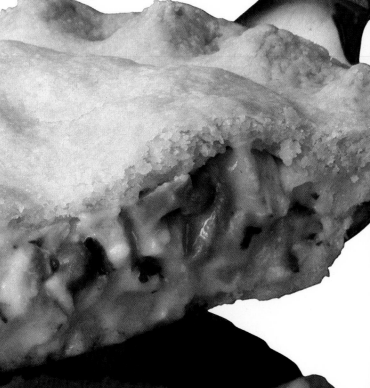

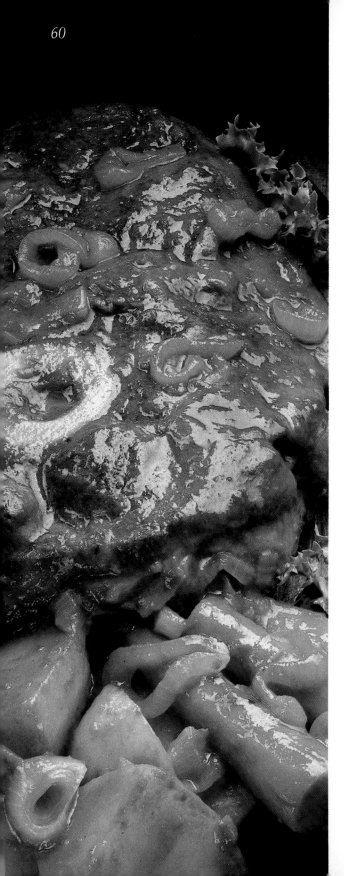

◄ Savory Pot Roast

6 tablespoons all-purpose flour, divided
1 teaspoon celery salt
1 teaspoon dried marjoram leaves
½ teaspoon dried summer savory leaves
⅛ teaspoon pepper
3½ to 4-pound beef chuck roast
¼ cup Crisco Oil
1 medium onion, thinly sliced
½ cup water
1 can (8 ounces) tomato sauce
2 teaspoons instant beef bouillon granules
4 medium carrots, cut into 3-inch pieces
4 medium potatoes, quartered
¼ cup cold water

Mix 4 tablespoons flour, celery salt, marjoram, summer savory and pepper in shallow baking dish. Coat roast evenly with flour mixture. Heat Crisco Oil in Dutch oven. Add roast and any remaining flour mixture. Brown over medium-high heat. Add onion, ½ cup water, tomato sauce and bouillon granules. Cover. Reduce heat. Simmer about 2 hours. Add carrots and potatoes; re-cover. Simmer about 1 hour, or until vegetables are tender. Transfer roast and vegetables to serving platter, reserving cooking liquid in Dutch oven.

Place ¼ cup cold water in 1-cup measure or small bowl. Mix in remaining 2 tablespoons flour. Stir into reserved cooking liquid. Cook over medium-high heat, stirring constantly, until thickened and bubbly. Serve with beef and vegetables.

4 servings

Sauerbraten ▼

1 cup cider vinegar
½ cup dry red wine or beef broth
½ cup water
2 medium onions, thinly sliced
1 carrot, sliced
1 stalk celery, chopped
1 tablespoon salt
12 whole peppercorns
4 whole cloves
2 whole allspice
4-pound boneless beef rump roast
4 tablespoons all-purpose flour, divided
¼ cup Crisco Oil
⅓ cup cold water
1 tablespoon sugar
½ cup crushed gingersnap cookies

Mix vinegar, wine, ½ cup water, onions, carrot, celery, salt, peppercorns, cloves and allspice in large bowl or large plastic food storage bag. Add roast. Cover bowl or seal bag. Refrigerate 2 to 3 days, turning roast over each day.

Remove roast from marinade, reserving marinade. Pat roast dry with paper towels. Coat with 2 tablespoons flour. Heat Crisco Oil in Dutch oven. Add roast. Brown over medium-high heat. Pour reserved marinade over roast. Cover. Reduce heat. Simmer 2½ to 3 hours, or until meat is tender, turning roast over after half the time. Transfer roast to serving platter, reserving liquid and vegetables in Dutch oven.

Strain vegetables and liquid through wire sieve into large bowl, pressing vegetables to remove liquid. Discard vegetables. Skim and discard fat from liquid. Pour 3 cups liquid into saucepan. Discard remaining liquid. Heat liquid to boiling. Meanwhile, place ⅓ cup cold water in small bowl. Blend in sugar and remaining 2 tablespoons flour. Add to boiling liquid. Cook, stirring constantly, until mixture is thickened. Stir in gingersnaps. Cook 1 to 2 minutes longer, or until heated through. Serve with roast.

8 to 10 servings

Wine-Simmered Beef and Vegetables ▲

1½ to 2 pounds beef round steak
  6 tablespoons all-purpose flour,
      divided
 ½ teaspoon salt
 ¼ teaspoon pepper
  3 tablespoons Crisco Oil
  1 medium onion, thinly sliced and
      separated into rings
  1 medium green pepper, cored,
      seeded and sliced into rings
 ⅔ cup julienne carrot strips
 ½ teaspoon dried basil leaves
 ½ teaspoon dried marjoram leaves
 ⅔ cup white wine
 ⅔ cup cold water
 ½ teaspoon instant beef bouillon
      granules

Trim bone and fat from beef. Pound trimmed beef with meat mallet. Cut into serving-size pieces. Set aside. Mix 4 tablespoons flour, salt and pepper in large plastic food storage bag. Add beef. Shake to coat.

Heat Crisco Oil in large skillet. Add beef and any remaining flour mixture. Brown over medium-high heat. Layer onion, green pepper and carrots over beef. Sprinkle with basil and marjoram. Add wine. Heat to boiling. Cover. Reduce heat. Simmer about 1 hour, or until beef is tender. Transfer beef and vegetables to serving platter, reserving drippings in skillet.

Place cold water in 1-cup measure or small bowl. Blend in remaining 2 tablespoons flour. Stir flour mixture into drippings in skillet. Stir in bouillon granules. Cook over medium-high heat, stirring constantly, until thickened and bubbly. Serve with meat and vegetables.

Simmered Beef and Vegetables: Follow recipe above, substituting ⅔ cup water and ¾ teaspoon instant beef bouillon granules for wine.

4 to 6 servings

Fruited Stew ▼

¼ cup Crisco Oil
2 pounds beef round steak, cut into 1-inch pieces
1 medium onion, chopped
1 medium green pepper, cored, seeded and chopped
2 cloves garlic, minced
2 medium tomatoes, peeled, seeded and chopped
2 medium potatoes, cut into ½-inch cubes
2 medium sweet potatoes or yams, peeled and cut into ½-inch cubes
1½ cups water
2 teaspoons instant beef bouillon granules
1 teaspoon salt
½ teaspoon ground thyme
¼ teaspoon ground marjoram
2 medium zucchini, thinly sliced
2 medium apples, peeled, cored and chopped
2 medium peaches, peeled, pitted and chopped, or 1 can (16 ounces) peach halves, drained and chopped
1 can (8 ounces) whole kernel corn, drained

Heat Crisco Oil in Dutch oven. Add beef. Brown over medium-high heat. Remove beef with slotted spoon; set aside.

Add onion, green pepper and garlic to Crisco Oil. Sauté over moderate heat until onion is tender. Add tomatoes. Cook, stirring constantly, about 3 minutes. Stir in beef, potatoes, sweet potatoes, water, bouillon granules, salt, thyme and marjoram. Heat to boiling. Cover. Reduce heat. Simmer, stirring occasionally, 1 to 1½ hours, or until beef is tender. Stir in remaining ingredients; re-cover. Simmer about 15 minutes longer, or until apple is tender.

8 to 10 servings

Beef Burgundy

½ cup all-purpose flour
¾ teaspoon salt
¼ teaspoon pepper
1½ pounds beef round steak, cut into
    1-inch pieces
5 tablespoons Crisco Oil, divided
1½ cups water
1 cup Burgundy wine
1 medium onion, thinly sliced
½ cup snipped fresh parsley
2 cloves garlic, halved
2 bay leaves
1½ teaspoons instant beef bouillon
    granules
1 teaspoon dried thyme leaves
8 ounces fresh mushrooms, sliced
¼ cup sliced almonds
    Hot cooked rice or noodles

Mix flour, salt and pepper in large plastic food storage bag. Add beef. Shake to coat. Heat 4 tablespoons Crisco Oil in Dutch oven. Add beef and any remaining flour mixture. Brown over medium-high heat. Stir in water, wine, onion, parsley, garlic, bay leaves, bouillon granules and thyme. Heat to boiling. Cover. Reduce heat. Simmer 1½ to 2 hours, or until beef is tender, stirring occasionally. Stir in mushrooms; re-cover. Simmer 20 to 30 minutes longer, or until mushrooms are tender. Remove and discard garlic cloves and bay leaves.

Meanwhile, heat remaining 1 tablespoon Crisco Oil in small skillet. Add almonds. Cook over moderate heat, stirring constantly, until almonds are lightly browned. Stir into beef mixture just before serving. Serve with rice or noodles.

4 to 6 servings

Texas Chili

¼ cup all-purpose flour
1½ pounds beef stew meat, cut into
    ¾-inch cubes
5 tablespoons Crisco Oil, divided
1 medium onion, chopped
2 cloves garlic, minced
2 cans (16 ounces each) whole
    tomatoes, undrained, cut up
2 cans (16 ounces each) kidney beans,
    drained
1 can (8 ounces) tomato sauce
1 tablespoon chili powder
1 teaspoon dried crushed red pepper
    (optional)
¼ to ½ teaspoon ground cumin
¼ teaspoon ground oregano

Place flour in large plastic food storage bag. Add beef. Shake to coat. Heat 3 tablespoons Crisco Oil in large saucepan. Add beef and any remaining flour. Brown over medium-high heat. Remove beef from saucepan; set aside.

Heat remaining 2 tablespoons Crisco Oil in large saucepan. Add onion and garlic. Sauté over moderate heat until onion is tender. Stir in beef, tomatoes, kidney beans, tomato sauce, chili powder, red pepper (optional), cumin and oregano. Heat to boiling. Cover. Reduce heat. Simmer, stirring occasionally, about 1 hour. Uncover. Simmer, stirring occasionally, 30 to 60 minutes longer, or until beef is tender.

6 to 8 servings

Mexican Beef Stew ▼

2 tablespoons Crisco Oil
2 pounds beef stew meat, cut into
  1-inch cubes
1 medium onion, chopped
1 clove garlic, minced
1 can (16 ounces) whole tomatoes,
  undrained, cut up
1 jar (4 ounces) pimiento, drained
  and mashed
½ to 1 teaspoon ground cumin
½ teaspoon salt
¼ teaspoon pepper

Heat Crisco Oil in large skillet. Add beef. Brown over medium-high heat. Remove beef with slotted spoon; set aside. Add onion and garlic to Crisco Oil in skillet. Sauté over moderate heat until onion is tender. Stir in beef and remaining ingredients. Heat to boiling. Cover. Reduce heat. Simmer, stirring occasionally, about 2 hours, or until beef is tender. Add water during cooking if necessary.

6 to 8 servings

Beef and Bean Sprout Stir-Fry ▼

1 egg white, slightly beaten
5 teaspoons soy sauce, divided
3 teaspoons cornstarch, divided
⅛ teaspoon ground ginger
⅛ teaspoon garlic powder
⅛ teaspoon salt
   Dash white pepper
¾ to 1 pound boneless beef sirloin, cut into thin strips
½ cup cold water
1 tablespoon oyster sauce (optional)*
½ teaspoon instant chicken bouillon granules
4 tablespoons Crisco Oil, divided
1 cup sliced fresh mushrooms
½ cup green onion slices, 1-inch slices
1 can (14 ounces) bean sprouts, drained
½ cup sliced water chestnuts
   Hot cooked rice

Blend egg white, 2 teaspoons soy sauce, 1 teaspoon cornstarch, ginger, garlic powder, salt and pepper in medium mixing bowl. Add beef. Stir to coat. Cover and refrigerate 30 minutes.

Combine cold water, oyster sauce (optional), remaining 3 teaspoons soy sauce, remaining 2 teaspoons cornstarch, and bouillon granules in small mixing bowl. Mix well. Set aside.

Heat 2 tablespoons Crisco Oil in large skillet. Add beef mixture. Stir-fry over medium-high heat until beef is browned. Remove mixture from skillet; set aside. Heat remaining 2 tablespoons Crisco Oil in large skillet. Add mushrooms and onion. Stir-fry over medium-high heat 1 minute. Add bean sprouts and water chestnuts. Stir-fry 1 minute. Add cornstarch mixture and beef. Stir-fry until thickened and bubbly. Serve with rice and additional *soy sauce*, if desired.

Available in Oriental foods section of supermarket.

4 to 6 servings

Sukiyaki

¼ cup soy sauce
¼ cup chicken broth
1 tablespoon sugar
2 teaspoons cornstarch
4 tablespoons Crisco Oil, divided
¾ to 1 pound boneless beef sirloin,
    cut into thin strips
8 ounces fresh mushrooms, sliced
12 green onions, cut into 2-inch slices
1 large onion, quartered and sliced
1 can (8 ounces) sliced bamboo
    shoots, drained
8 ounces fresh spinach, washed,
    drained and torn into bite-size
    pieces
    Hot cooked rice

Blend soy sauce, chicken broth, sugar and cornstarch in small bowl. Set aside.

Heat 2 tablespoons Crisco Oil in large skillet. Add beef. Stir-fry over medium-high heat until browned. Remove beef and drippings from skillet; set aside.

Heat remaining 2 tablespoons Crisco Oil in skillet. Add mushrooms, green onions, onion and bamboo shoots. Stir-fry over medium-high heat about 4 minutes, or until onion is tender-crisp. Stir in soy sauce mixture. Cover. Cook over moderate heat 3 minutes. Stir in spinach; re-cover. Cook 2 minutes longer. Add beef. Stir-fry 1 to 2 minutes, or until hot. Serve with rice.

4 to 6 servings

Spaghetti Sauce

1 pound ground beef
¼ cup Crisco Oil
½ cup chopped carrot
½ cup chopped celery
⅓ cup chopped onion
2 cloves garlic, minced
1 can (16 ounces) whole tomatoes,
    undrained
1 can (10¾ ounces) condensed tomato
    soup
1 can (6 ounces) tomato paste
¼ cup sliced pimiento-stuffed green
    olives
2 teaspoons sugar
1½ teaspoons Italian seasoning
¾ teaspoon salt
½ teaspoon dried crushed red pepper
1 bay leaf
    Hot cooked spaghetti

Place ground beef in large saucepan. Brown over medium-high heat. Drain. Remove beef from saucepan; set aside.

Heat Crisco Oil in large saucepan. Add carrot, celery, onion and garlic. Sauté over moderate heat until carrot is tender. Add beef and remaining ingredients except spaghetti, stirring to blend and break apart tomatoes. Heat to boiling. Cover. Reduce heat. Simmer, stirring occasionally, 45 minutes to 1 hour, or until flavors are blended. Remove and discard bay leaf. Serve with spaghetti.

6 to 8 servings

Layered Beef and Eggplant Bake ▲

1 recipe Fried Eggplant, page 95
1 pound ground beef
1 can (16 ounces) whole tomatoes, drained
½ cup sliced fresh mushrooms
1 can (6 ounces) tomato paste
¼ cup chopped onion
¼ cup grated Parmesan cheese
1 teaspoon dried basil leaves
¾ teaspoon salt
½ teaspoon dried oregano leaves
1 clove garlic, minced
⅛ teaspoon pepper
2½ cups shredded mozzarella cheese

Prepare Fried Eggplant as directed. Set aside.

Place ground beef in large skillet. Brown over medium-high heat. Drain.

Add remaining ingredients except mozzarella cheese. Stir to blend and break apart tomatoes. Cover. Reduce heat. Simmer about 10 minutes, or until flavors are blended.

Preheat oven to 350°F. Layer half the eggplant, half the ground beef mixture and 1 cup mozzarella cheese in 8-inch square baking dish. Repeat ground beef and mozzarella cheese layers. Top with remaining eggplant. Sprinkle with remaining ½ cup mozzarella cheese. Cover dish with aluminum foil. Bake at 350°F, about 15 minutes. Remove aluminum foil and bake 10 to 15 minutes longer, or until bubbly.

4 to 6 servings

Ground Beef Stroganoff

1 pound ground beef
2 tablespoons Crisco Oil
⅔ cup chopped onion
1 clove garlic, minced
1 can (10¾ ounces) condensed cream
　　of mushroom soup
1 cup water
1 jar (4½ ounces) whole mushrooms,
　　drained
1 teaspoon dried parsley flakes
1 teaspoon paprika
1 teaspoon Worcestershire sauce
¼ teaspoon salt
¼ teaspoon pepper
½ cup dairy sour cream
　　Hot cooked noodles

Place ground beef in medium skillet.
Brown over medium-high heat. Drain.
Remove beef from skillet; set aside.

Heat Crisco Oil in medium skillet. Add
onion and garlic. Sauté over moderate
heat until onion is tender. Add ground
beef, soup, water, mushrooms, parsley
flakes, paprika, Worcestershire sauce,
salt and pepper. Mix well. Heat to
boiling. Reduce heat to medium-low.
Cook 15 minutes. Reduce heat to low.
Blend in sour cream. Cook 1 to 2
minutes longer. Serve with noodles.

4 to 6 servings

Swedish Meatballs

1 pound lean ground beef
½ pound ground pork
⅔ cup milk
1 slice soft bread, torn into small
　　pieces
½ cup graham cracker crumbs
¼ cup finely-chopped onion
1 egg, slightly beaten
1 tablespoon packed brown sugar
1 teaspoon salt
¼ teaspoon ground allspice
¼ teaspoon ground nutmeg
⅛ teaspoon ground ginger
⅛ teaspoon ground cloves
⅛ teaspoon pepper
　　Crisco Oil for frying
¼ cup water

Combine ground beef, ground pork,
milk, bread, cracker crumbs, onion,
egg, brown sugar, salt, allspice,
nutmeg, ginger, cloves and pepper in
medium mixing bowl. Mix well. Shape
into 1¼-inch balls.

Preheat oven to 300°F. Heat about 2
tablespoons Crisco Oil in medium
skillet. Brown a few meatballs at a time
over medium-high heat, adding more
Crisco Oil as needed. Place browned
meatballs in 12 × 8-inch baking dish.
Add water. Cover dish with aluminum
foil. Bake at 300°F, 45 to 55 minutes, or
until firm.

6 servings

Beef and Bean Chimichangas ▼

1 pound ground beef
2 tablespoons Crisco Oil
1 medium onion, chopped
2 cloves garlic, minced
1 can (16 ounces) whole tomatoes,
   drained, cut up
⅓ cup salsa sauce
1½ teaspoons chili powder
¾ teaspoon ground coriander
½ teaspoon ground thyme
½ teaspoon salt
⅛ teaspoon cayenne
⅛ teaspoon ground cumin
1 cup refried beans
   Crisco Oil for frying
   Six 8-inch flour tortillas
¾ cup shredded Monterey Jack cheese

Place ground beef in medium skillet. Brown over medium-high heat. Drain. Remove beef from skillet; set aside. Place 2 tablespoons Crisco Oil in medium skillet. Add onion and garlic.

Sauté over moderate heat until onion is tender. Stir in ground beef, tomatoes, salsa sauce, chili powder, coriander, thyme, salt, cayenne and cumin. Cook over medium-low heat, stirring occasionally, 10 to 15 minutes, or until mixture is thickened. Remove from heat. Stir in refried beans.

Heat 2 inches Crisco Oil in deep-fryer or large saucepan to 375°F. Meanwhile, place ½ cup beef mixture in center of each tortilla. Fold opposite sides of tortilla to center over beef mixture. Fold ends toward center; secure with wooden pick.

Fry 1 or 2 chimichangas at a time 1½ to 2 minutes, or until golden brown. Drain on paper towels. Sprinkle top of each chimichanga with 2 tablespoons Monterey Jack cheese. Serve immediately with *salsa sauce,* if desired.

6 servings

How to Assemble Chimichangas

Spoon filling onto center of each tortilla. Fold two sides of tortilla over filling. Fold ends toward center. Secure ends with wooden picks.

Liver and Onions

½ cup all-purpose flour
1 teaspoon ground sage
¾ teaspoon salt
½ teaspoon paprika
⅛ teaspoon cayenne
1 pound beef liver, membrane removed, cut into 4 × 1 × ¼-inch strips
¼ cup Crisco Oil
1 large onion, thinly sliced and separated into rings
⅛ teaspoon instant minced garlic
2 tablespoons snipped fresh parsley
¼ cup white wine or chicken broth
1 tablespoon lemon juice

Mix flour, sage, salt, paprika and cayenne in large plastic food storage bag. Add liver. Shake to coat. Remove liver from bag; set aside.

Heat Crisco Oil in medium skillet. Add onion and garlic. Sauté over moderate heat until onion is tender. Push to one side of skillet. Add liver. Fry 6 to 8 minutes, or until no longer pink, turning over 1 or 2 times.

Stir together liver and onion. Sprinkle with parsley. Add wine and lemon juice. Cook, stirring constantly, 1 to 2 minutes longer.

4 servings

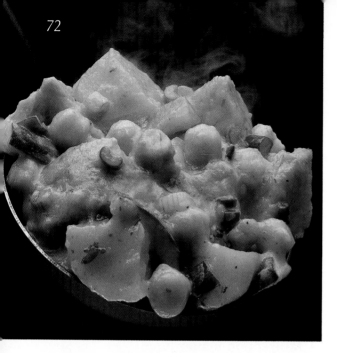

Herb-Marinated Pork Roast

3½ to 4-pound bone-in pork loin roast
 1 small onion, chopped
 ½ cup Crisco Oil
 3 tablespoons cider vinegar
 1 tablespoon lemon juice
 1 teaspoon dried oregano leaves
 2 cloves garlic, minced
 ½ teaspoon dried rosemary leaves
 ¼ teaspoon dried dill weed
 ¼ teaspoon salt
 ¼ teaspoon pepper

Place roast in large bowl or large heavy plastic food storage bag. Blend remaining ingredients. Pour over roast. Cover dish or seal bag. Refrigerate 8 hours or overnight, turning roast over occasionally.

Preheat oven to 325°F. Remove roast from marinade. Discard marinade. Place roast in roasting pan. Roast at 325°F, 2 to 3 hours, or until internal temperature registers 170°F. Let stand 15 minutes before carving.

6 to 8 servings

◄ Autumn Stew

 ¼ cup all-purpose flour
 2 teaspoons dried parsley flakes
 ½ teaspoon dried thyme leaves
 ½ teaspoon salt
 ½ teaspoon ground ginger
 ¼ teaspoon ground nutmeg
 ¼ teaspoon pepper
 2 pounds pork stew meat, cut into
   1½-inch cubes
 3 tablespoons Crisco Oil
 1 can (16 ounces) pumpkin
 1 can (15 ounces) garbanzo beans,
   drained
 2 cups water
 1 medium sweet potato, peeled and
   cut into ¾-inch cubes
 ½ cup chopped green onion
 1 tablespoon packed brown sugar
 2 teaspoons instant chicken bouillon
   granules
 1 bay leaf
 1 medium zucchini, cut into julienne
   strips

Mix flour, parsley flakes, thyme, salt, ginger, nutmeg and pepper in large plastic food storage bag. Add pork. Shake to coat.

Heat Crisco Oil in Dutch oven. Add pork and any remaining flour mixture. Brown over medium-high heat. Stir in remaining ingredients except zucchini. Heat to boiling. Cover. Reduce heat. Simmer, stirring occasionally, 1½ to 2 hours. Add zucchini; re-cover. Simmer 30 minutes longer, or until pork is tender. Remove and discard bay leaf.

Rutabaga Variation: Follow recipe above, substituting 1⅓ cups cubed rutabaga (½-inch cubes) for sweet potato.

8 to 10 servings

Sweet-and-Sour Pork

½ cup all-purpose flour
1 teaspoon salt
½ teaspoon baking powder
½ cup cold water
1 pound lean boneless pork, cut into 1-inch cubes
1 can (20 ounces) pineapple chunks
2 tablespoons white vinegar
1 tablespoon cornstarch
  Crisco Oil for frying
3 carrots, cut into thin diagonal slices
1 green pepper, seeded, cored and cut into 1-inch pieces
3 tablespoons packed brown sugar
  Hot cooked rice

Mix flour, salt and baking powder in medium mixing bowl. Blend in cold water. Add pork. Stir to coat. Set aside. Drain pineapple chunks, reserving juice. Set aside pineapple chunks. Blend reserved pineapple juice, vinegar and cornstarch in small bowl. Set aside.

Heat 1 inch Crisco Oil in Dutch oven to 375°F. Remove half the pork from batter with slotted spoon; add to Crisco Oil. Fry 3 to 5 minutes, or until golden brown. Drain on paper towels. Repeat with remaining pork. Discard Crisco Oil, reserving about 1 tablespoon in Dutch oven. Add carrots. Stir-fry over moderate heat 2 to 3 minutes, or until tender-crisp. Add green pepper. Stir-fry 2 to 3 minutes longer. Add pineapple juice mixture, pineapple chunks and brown sugar. Heat to boiling, stirring constantly. Cook and stir until mixture is clear and thickened. Stir in pork. Cook about 3 minutes, or until hot. Serve with rice.

4 to 6 servings

Oven Barbecued Ribs ▼

¼ cup Crisco Oil
3 to 4 pounds pork spareribs, cut into serving-size pieces
½ cup chopped onion
⅓ cup chopped celery
¼ cup grated carrot
⅓ cup catsup
¼ cup packed brown sugar
1 tablespoon prepared mustard
1½ teaspoons chili powder
½ teaspoon salt
¼ teaspoon cayenne

Preheat oven to 350°F. Heat Crisco Oil in large skillet. Add ribs. Brown over medium-high heat. Remove ribs from skillet; set aside. Discard drippings, reserving 2 tablespoons in skillet. Arrange ribs in 13 × 9-inch baking dish. Cover dish with aluminum foil. Bake at 350°F, 1 hour.

Meanwhile, heat 2 tablespoons reserved drippings in skillet. Add onion, celery and carrot. Sauté over moderate heat until tender. Stir in remaining ingredients. Simmer, stirring occasionally, about 5 minutes. Drain ribs. Baste generously with sauce. Re-cover with aluminum foil. Bake at 350°F, 30 to 60 minutes, or until tender.

4 servings

Herbed Pork Sauté ▼

¼ cup all-purpose flour
½ teaspoon dried basil leaves
½ teaspoon dried marjoram leaves
½ teaspoon salt
¼ teaspoon pepper
1 to 1½ pounds butterflied pork
chops, cut into thin strips
4 tablespoons Crisco Oil, divided
1 teaspoon instant chicken bouillon
granules
1 teaspoon instant beef bouillon
granules
1 cup hot water
½ cup coarsley-chopped onion
½ cup chopped carrot
1 package (10 ounces) frozen Brussels
sprouts
Hot mashed potatoes (optional)

Mix flour, basil, marjoram, salt and
pepper in large plastic food storage bag.
Add pork. Shake to coat.

Heat 3 tablespoons Crisco Oil in large
skillet. Add pork and any remaining
flour mixture. Brown over medium-high
heat. Remove pork and drippings from
skillet; set aside.

Dissolve chicken and beef bouillon
granules in hot water. Set aside. Heat
remaining 1 tablespoon Crisco Oil in
large skillet. Add onion and carrot.
Sauté over moderate heat until tender.
Stir in pork, bouillon mixture and
Brussels sprouts. Heat to boiling. Cover.
Cook over moderate heat, stirring
occasionally, about 10 minutes, or until
Brussels sprouts are tender and pork is
no longer pink. Serve with mashed
potatoes (optional).

4 to 6 servings

Dijon Breaded Pork Chops

¾ cup finely-crushed saltine crackers
½ teaspoon salt
½ teaspoon ground thyme
¼ teaspoon pepper
⅛ to ¼ teaspoon ground sage
1 egg
1 tablespoon Dijon mustard
4 pork chops, ½ inch thick
¼ cup Crisco Oil

Mix cracker crumbs, salt, thyme, pepper
and sage in shallow dish or on sheet of
waxed paper. Set aside. Blend egg and
mustard in shallow dish. Dip each chop
in egg mixture, then in cracker mixture
to coat.

Heat Crisco Oil in large skillet. Add
chops. Fry over moderate heat 16 to 20
minutes, or until pork is no longer
pink, turning over once.

2 to 4 servings

Crispy Fried Pork and Apples

6 butterflied pork chops, ½ inch thick
1 large apple, peeled and cored
2 eggs
2 tablespoons half-and-half
1 cup unseasoned dry bread crumbs
1 teaspoon ground ginger
¾ teaspoon salt
½ teaspoon ground coriander (optional)
¼ teaspoon ground allspice
  Crisco Oil for frying

Pound each chop with meat mallet. Slice apple into 6 rings. Blend eggs and half-and-half in small mixing bowl. Mix bread crumbs, ginger, salt, coriander (optional) and allspice in shallow dish or on sheet of waxed paper. Set aside.

Heat 2 to 3 inches Crisco Oil in deep-fryer or large saucepan to 350°F. Dip pork and apple rings in egg mixture, then in bread crumb mixture to coat. Fry 2 or 3 pieces pork at a time 2 to 3 minutes, or until deep golden brown. Drain on paper towels. Fry apple rings 2 to 3 minutes, or until deep golden brown. Drain on paper towels.

6 servings

Fruit-Stuffed Pork Chops

1 can (16 ounces) pitted tart cherries, drained
½ cup chopped apple
¼ cup raisins
¼ cup chopped dried apricots
1 teaspoon ground cinnamon
½ teaspoon instant chicken bouillon granules
½ teaspoon salt
⅛ teaspoon ground allspice
⅛ teaspoon ground cloves
⅛ teaspoon pepper
5 tablespoons Crisco Oil, divided
⅓ cup chopped onion
1 cup herb-seasoned stuffing mix
¼ cup packed brown sugar
4 pork chops with pocket, 1 inch thick

Preheat oven to 350°F. Mix cherries, apple, raisins, apricots, cinnamon, bouillon granules, salt, allspice, cloves and pepper in medium mixing bowl. Set aside.

Heat 1 tablespoon Crisco Oil in small saucepan. Add onion. Sauté over moderate heat until tender. Stir in stuffing mix, brown sugar and cherry mixture. Remove from heat. Fill each chop pocket with one-fourth of stuffing. Secure edges with wooden picks.

Heat remaining 4 tablespoons Crisco Oil in large skillet. Add chops. Brown over medium-high heat. Place chops in 8-inch square baking dish. Cover dish with aluminum foil. Bake at 350°F, about 40 minutes, or until pork is no longer pink. Remove wooden picks before serving.

4 servings

Hungarian Pork Dinner ▼

¼ cup all-purpose flour
¾ teaspoon lemon pepper seasoning
4 pork shoulder chops, ½ inch thick
3 tablespoons Crisco Oil
2 teaspoons grated lemon peel
2 teaspoons dried parsley flakes
½ teaspoon caraway seed
½ teaspoon salt
¼ teaspoon pepper
4 cups sliced white potatoes
½ teaspoon instant chicken bouillon granules
⅓ cup hot water

Preheat oven to 325°F. Lightly oil 13 × 9-inch baking pan with Crisco Oil. Set aside. Mix flour and lemon pepper seasoning in large plastic food storage bag. Add chops. Shake to coat. Heat Crisco Oil in large skillet. Add chops and any remaining flour mixture. Brown over medium-high heat. Set aside.

Mix lemon peel, parsley flakes, caraway seed, salt and pepper in small bowl. Spread half the potatoes in prepared pan. Sprinkle with half the lemon peel mixture. Spread with remaining potatoes and remaining lemon peel mixture. Dissolve bouillon granules in hot water. Pour over potatoes. Top with chops. Cover dish with aluminum foil. Bake at 325°F, 30 to 45 minutes, or until chops are no longer pink and potatoes are tender.

4 servings

Ham Patties

5 tablespoons Crisco Oil, divided
¼ cup chopped onion
2 tablespoons chopped green pepper
½ pound ground fully-cooked ham
¼ pound ground pork
1 egg, slightly beaten
½ cup unseasoned dry bread crumbs, divided
2 teaspoons dry mustard
Mustard Sauce, page 23 (optional)

Heat 2 tablespoons Crisco Oil in large skillet. Add onion and green pepper. Sauté over moderate heat until tender. Transfer to medium mixing bowl. Add ground ham, ground pork, egg, ¼ cup bread crumbs and mustard. Mix well. Set aside.

Spread remaining ¼ cup bread crumbs on plate or sheet of waxed paper. Place one-fourth ham mixture on bread crumbs. Flatten to form ½-inch thick patty. Coat both sides with bread crumbs, pressing to coat thoroughly. Repeat with remaining ham mixture.

Heat remaining 3 tablespoons Crisco Oil in large skillet. Add ham patties. Fry over moderate heat 8 to 10 minutes, or until firm, turning over once. Serve with Mustard Sauce (optional).

4 servings

Roast Leg of Lamb

  1 teaspoon salt
½ teaspoon pepper
  5-pound leg of lamb
  3 cloves garlic, slivered
¼ cup Crisco Oil
  2 tablespoons lemon juice
½ teaspoon dried rosemary leaves

Preheat oven to 325°F. Rub salt and pepper on lamb. Cut slits in lamb and insert garlic slivers. Place leg, fat-side-up, in roasting pan. Blend Crisco Oil and lemon juice in small bowl. Brush onto lamb. Sprinkle lamb with rosemary. Roast at 325°F, about 3 hours, or until internal temperature registers 170° to 180°F, brushing with lemon juice mixture several times. Cover with aluminum foil and let stand 15 to 20 minutes before carving.

6 to 8 servings

◄ Marinated Lamb Kabobs

  6 tablespoons Crisco Oil
  2 teaspoons dried rosemary leaves
  1 teaspoon dried thyme leaves
  3 cloves garlic, minced
½ teaspoon dried oregano leaves
  6 tablespoons lime juice
½ teaspoon sugar
½ teaspoon salt
  1 pound boneless leg of lamb or lamb
      shoulder, cut into 1-inch cubes
  8 large mushroom caps
  4 small onions, cut into thirds
  1 medium green pepper, cored, seeded
      and cut into 16 pieces

Heat Crisco Oil in small skillet. Add rosemary, thyme, garlic and oregano. Sauté over moderate heat until garlic is lightly browned. Remove from heat. Stir in lime juice, sugar and salt. Transfer mixture to large plastic food storage bag. Add lamb and mushroom caps. Seal bag and refrigerate at least 8 hours, turning bag over occasionally. Remove lamb and mushroom caps from marinade, reserving marinade.

Skewer lamb, mushroom caps, onion and green pepper on four 12-inch skewers. Set oven to broil and/or 550°F. Place kabobs on broiler pan. Brush with reserved marinade. Broil 3 to 4 inches from heat, 10 to 20 minutes, or until lamb is desired doneness, turning kabobs over once. Serve with *hot cooked rice*, if desired.

4 servings

Lamb Stew

2 tablespoons Crisco Oil
2 pounds boneless leg of lamb or
   lamb shoulder, cut into 1½-inch
   cubes
5 medium white potatoes, thinly
   sliced
3 medium onions, thinly sliced and
   separated into rings
2 tablespoons dried parsley flakes
1 teaspoon salt
1 teaspoon dried thyme leaves
½ teaspoon pepper
3 cups water
1 bay leaf

Heat Crisco Oil in Dutch oven. Add
lamb. Brown over medium-high heat.
Spread potatoes and onions over lamb.
Sprinkle with parsley flakes, salt, thyme
and pepper. Add water and bay leaf.
Heat to boiling. Cover. Reduce heat.
Simmer, stirring occasionally, 1½ to 2
hours, or until lamb is tender. Remove
and discard bay leaf.

8 to 10 servings

Lamb Pilaf ▼

3 tablespoons Crisco Oil
1 pound boneless leg of lamb or
   lamb shoulder, cut into ¾-inch
   cubes
½ cup chopped onion
⅓ cup chopped green pepper
2½ cups hot water
1½ cups uncooked long grain rice
2 teaspoons dried parsley flakes
2 teaspoons instant chicken bouillon
   granules
1½ teaspoons curry powder
1 bay leaf
¼ teaspoon pepper
¼ teaspoon salt

Heat Crisco Oil in medium skillet. Add
lamb. Brown over medium-high heat.
Remove with slotted spoon; set aside.
Add onion and green pepper to
drippings in skillet. Cook over moderate
heat, stirring occasionally, until tender.
Stir in lamb and remaining ingredients.
Heat to boiling. Cover. Reduce heat.
Simmer 20 to 25 minutes, or until lamb
and rice are tender and liquid is
absorbed. Fluff with fork before serving.

4 to 6 servings

Lemon and Garlic Lamb Chops ▼

1 tablespoon all-purpose flour
1 tablespoon grated lemon peel
½ teaspoon garlic powder
¼ teaspoon salt
⅛ teaspoon pepper
4 lamb shoulder chops
¼ cup Crisco Oil

Mix flour, lemon peel, garlic powder, salt and pepper in large plastic food storage bag. Add chops. Shake to coat. Set aside.

Heat Crisco Oil in large skillet. Add chops and any remaining flour mixture. Fry over medium-high heat about 10 minutes, or until chops are golden brown, turning over once. Drain on paper towels.

4 servings

Lamb Patties

3 tablespoons Crisco Oil, divided
¼ cup chopped onion
¼ cup snipped fresh parsley
1 clove garlic, minced
¾ pound ground lamb
¼ pound ground beef
½ teaspoon dried dill weed
½ teaspoon salt
¼ teaspoon dried rosemary leaves, crushed
¼ teaspoon pepper

Heat 1 tablespoon Crisco Oil in large skillet. Add onion, parsley and garlic. Sauté over moderate heat until onion is tender. Transfer mixture to medium mixing bowl. Add remaining ingredients. Mix well. Shape into four ½-inch thick patties.

Heat remaining 2 tablespoons Crisco Oil in large skillet. Add patties. Fry over moderate heat 8 to 10 minutes, or until desired doneness, turning over once.

4 servings

Country-Style Veal

¼ cup all-purpose flour
3 tablespoons water
2 tablespoons white wine
1½ teaspoons instant beef bouillon
    granules
½ teaspoon dried basil leaves
½ teaspoon dried thyme leaves
¼ teaspoon dried marjoram leaves
¼ teaspoon salt
⅛ teaspoon pepper
⅛ teaspoon garlic powder
3 tablespoons Crisco Oil
1 to 1½ pounds veal round steak, cut
    into serving-size pieces
1 medium onion, halved and
    thinly sliced
8 ounces whole fresh mushrooms
2 tomatoes, peeled, seeded and cut
    into chunks
2 slices lemon
1 bay leaf

Mix flour, water, wine, bouillon granules, basil, thyme, marjoram, salt, pepper and garlic powder in small mixing bowl. Set aside. Heat Crisco Oil in large skillet. Add veal. Fry over medium-high heat until no longer pink.

Remove veal from skillet; set aside. Add onion to drippings in skillet. Sauté over moderate heat until tender. Reduce heat to low. Stir in remaining ingredients and the veal. Add flour mixture. Stir. Cover. Simmer, stirring once, 25 to 30 minutes, or until mushrooms are tender. Remove and discard bay leaf.

4 to 6 servings

Stuffed Veal Cutlets

1 package (3 ounces) cream cheese, softened
2 teaspoons grated Parmesan cheese
1 teaspoon Dijon mustard
½ teaspoon dried parsley flakes
⅛ teaspoon garlic powder
½ cup all-purpose flour
¼ teaspoon salt
⅛ teaspoon pepper
1 cup seasoned dry bread crumbs
2 eggs, slightly beaten
8 thin slices fully-cooked ham
8 veal cutlets, pounded thin
8 thin slices Swiss cheese (each about 4 inches square), halved
Crisco Oil for frying

Combine cream cheese, Parmesan cheese, mustard, parsley flakes and garlic powder in small mixing bowl. Mix well. Set aside. Mix flour, salt and pepper in shallow dish. Place bread crumbs on sheet of waxed paper. Place eggs in another shallow dish. Set aside.

Place ham slice on top of each cutlet. Trim ham to within ½ inch of cutlet edge. Spread each ham slice with one-eighth of cream cheese mixture (a scant tablespoon). Top each with 2 pieces Swiss cheese. Brush top edges of cutlets with egg. Fold in half. Press and pound edges of cutlets together to seal. Carefully coat both sides with flour mixture. Dip stuffed cutlets in egg, then in bread crumbs, pressing to coat thoroughly. Cover and refrigerate about 1 hour.

Heat 2 inches Crisco Oil in deep-fryer or large saucepan to 350°F. Fry 1 stuffed cutlet at a time, about 2½ minutes, or until deep golden brown, turning over once. Drain on paper towels.

4 to 8 servings

Veal Parmesan

Sauce:
2 tablespoons Crisco Oil
1 small onion, thinly sliced and separated into rings
½ cup chopped green pepper
1 clove garlic, minced
1 can (15 ounces) tomato sauce
2 tablespoons white wine
¾ teaspoon dried basil leaves
½ teaspoon sugar
¼ teaspoon fennel seed
¼ teaspoon salt
⅛ teaspoon pepper

1 cup seasoned dry bread crumbs
¾ cup grated Parmesan cheese, divided
¼ teaspoon pepper
2 eggs, slightly beaten
1 pound veal cutlets, ¼ inch thick
Crisco Oil for frying

For sauce, heat Crisco Oil in medium saucepan. Add onion, green pepper and garlic. Sauté over moderate heat until tender. Stir in remaining sauce ingredients. Heat to boiling. Reduce heat. Simmer, uncovered, 30 minutes, or until sauce thickens.

Meanwhile, mix bread crumbs, ¼ cup Parmesan cheese and pepper in shallow dish. Place eggs in another shallow dish. Dip veal in eggs, then in bread crumb mixture to coat.

Preheat oven to 350°F. Heat ¼ inch Crisco Oil in large skillet. Add veal. Fry over moderate heat 3 to 4 minutes, or until golden brown, turning over once. Drain on paper towels. Arrange cutlets in 13 × 9-inch baking dish. Pour sauce over veal. Sprinkle with remaining ½ cup Parmesan cheese. Bake at 350°F, 15 to 20 minutes or until cheese melts.

4 to 6 servings

◄ Halibut Provençale

6 tablespoons Crisco Oil, divided
½ cup chopped onion
½ cup chopped green pepper
2 cloves garlic, minced
1 cup sliced fresh mushrooms
1 large tomato, peeled, seeded and chopped
3 pounds halibut fillets, cut into serving-size pieces
¾ cup white wine*
2 tablespoons snipped fresh parsley
2 small bay leaves

Heat 2 tablespoons Crisco Oil in small skillet. Add onion, green pepper and garlic. Sauté over moderate heat until tender. Stir in mushrooms and tomato. Set aside.

Heat remaining 4 tablespoons Crisco Oil in large skillet. Add fish. Fry over medium-high heat 4 minutes, turning over once. Remove from heat. Spread vegetable mixture on fish. Add wine, parsley and bay leaves. Cover. Cook over low heat 10 to 15 minutes, or until fish flakes easily with fork. Remove and discard bay leaves.

*For milder flavor, substitute ½ cup water and ¼ cup white wine for ¾ cup white wine.

12 servings

Fish and Chip Fillets

1 bag (4 ounces) potato chips, finely crushed (about 1¼ cups)
½ teaspoon onion powder
½ teaspoon salt
¼ teaspoon paprika
¼ teaspoon pepper
1 can (5.3 ounces) evaporated milk
1 pound fish fillets, ½ inch thick, cut into serving-size pieces
Crisco Oil for frying

Mix potato chip crumbs, onion powder, salt, paprika and pepper in shallow dish or on sheet of waxed paper. Set aside. Pour evaporated milk in another shallow dish. Dip fish in evaporated milk, then in potato chip mixture, pressing to coat thoroughly.

Heat ⅛ inch Crisco Oil in large skillet. Add fish. Fry 5 to 8 minutes, or until fish flakes easily with fork, turning over once. Drain on paper towels.

4 servings

Lemony Fish Fillets

1¼ cups crushed cornflakes
2 teaspoons lemon pepper seasoning
¼ to ½ teaspoon dried dill weed
⅛ teaspoon garlic powder
½ cup buttermilk
1 egg
1 pound fish fillets, ½ inch thick, cut into serving-size pieces
Crisco Oil for frying

Mix cornflake crumbs, lemon pepper seasoning, dill weed and garlic powder in shallow dish or on sheet of waxed paper. Set aside. Blend buttermilk and egg in medium mixing bowl. Dip fish in buttermilk mixture, then in cornflake mixture to coat.

Heat ⅛ inch Crisco Oil in large skillet. Add fish. Fry 5 to 8 minutes, or until fish flakes easily with fork, turning over once. Drain on paper towels.

4 servings

Tangy Baked Fish Fillets

¼ cup Crisco Oil
2 medium onions, thinly sliced and separated into rings
1½ to 2 pounds fish fillets, ½ inch thick, cut into serving-size pieces
½ teaspoon salt
¼ teaspoon pepper
3 medium tomatoes, seeded and chopped
2 lemons, thinly sliced
1 bay leaf
1 tablespoon white vinegar
1 tablespoon sugar

Preheat oven to 325°F. Heat Crisco Oil in deep skillet with ovenproof handle. Add onion. Sauté over moderate heat until tender. Remove from heat. Arrange fish on onion. Sprinkle with salt and pepper. Top with tomatoes and lemons. Add bay leaf. Sprinkle with vinegar and sugar. Cover. Bake at 325°F, 45 minutes to 1 hour, or until fish flakes easily with fork. Remove and discard bay leaf.

6 to 8 servings

Salmon Patties ▼

¼ cup Homemade Mayonnaise,
   page 44
5 tablespoons Crisco Oil, divided
2 tablespoons finely-chopped onion
2 tablespoons finely-chopped celery
2 tablespoons finely-chopped green
   pepper
1 can (7¾ ounces) salmon, drained,
   cleaned and flaked
1 egg
½ cup seasoned dry bread crumbs
1 tablespoon chili sauce
1 teaspoon lemon juice
¼ teaspoon pepper
½ cup instant mashed potato flakes

Prepare Homemade Mayonnaise as directed. Cover and refrigerate.

Heat 1 tablespoon Crisco Oil in small skillet. Add onion, celery and green pepper. Sauté over moderate heat until tender. Transfer to medium mixing bowl. Add salmon, egg, bread crumbs, ¼ cup mayonnaise, chili sauce, lemon juice and pepper. Mix well. Set aside.

Place potato flakes in shallow dish or on sheet of waxed paper. Place scant ½ cup salmon mixture on potato flakes. Flatten to form a patty ¾ inch thick. Coat both sides with potato flakes. Repeat with remaining salmon mixture to form 4 patties.

Heat remaining 4 tablespoons Crisco Oil in large skillet. Add patties. Fry over moderate heat 6 to 8 minutes, or until golden brown and firm, turning over once. Drain on paper towels.

Tuna Patties: Follow recipe above, substituting 1 can (6½ ounces) tuna, drained and flaked, for salmon.

Crab Cakes: Follow recipe above, substituting 1 can (6 ounces) crab meat, drained, cleaned and flaked, for salmon.

4 servings

Salmon Steaks with Cucumber Sauce ▼

- 4 salmon steaks, 1 inch thick
- 2 tablespoons Crisco Oil
- ¾ cup peeled, seeded and chopped cucumber
- ¼ cup finely-chopped celery
- 2 tablespoons chopped green onion
- 2 tablespoons all-purpose flour
- 1 teaspoon instant chicken bouillon granules
- ⅛ teaspoon pepper
- 1 cup half-and-half
- 1 egg yolk, slightly beaten

Set oven to broil and/or 550°F. Place salmon steaks on broiler pan. Broil 3 to 4 inches from heat, 10 to 15 minutes, or until fish flakes easily with fork, turning over once.

Meanwhile, heat Crisco Oil in small saucepan. Add cucumber and celery. Sauté over moderate heat until tender-crisp. Add onion. Sauté 30 seconds longer. Stir in flour, bouillon granules and pepper. Blend in half-and-half. Cook, stirring constantly, 5 to 7 minutes, or until thickened and bubbly. Blend small amount of hot mixture into egg yolk. Add back to hot mixture. Cook, stirring constantly, 1 minute. Serve with salmon.

4 servings

Crispy Fried Catfish

- 1 cup white or yellow cornmeal
- 1 teaspoon salt
- ¼ to ½ teaspoon cayenne
- 1 can (5.3 ounces) evaporated milk
- 1½ to 2 pounds catfish fillets
  Crisco Oil for frying

Mix cornmeal, salt and cayenne in shallow bowl or on sheet of waxed paper. Set aside. Place milk in another shallow dish. Dip fish in milk, then in cornmeal mixture to coat.

Heat 2 to 3 inches Crisco Oil in deep-fryer or large saucepan to 375°F. Fry a few pieces fish at a time, 3 to 4 minutes, or until light golden brown. Drain on paper towels. Repeat with remaining fish. Serve immediately or keep warm in 175°F oven.

6 to 8 servings

Shrimp Creole ▼

¼ cup Crisco Oil
3 tablespoons all-purpose flour
⅓ cup chopped onion
¼ cup chopped celery
¼ cup chopped green pepper
1 can (16 ounces) whole tomatoes,
    undrained
1 can (15 ounces) tomato sauce
1 thin slice lemon
2 teaspoons packed brown sugar
1 teaspoon chili powder
½ teaspoon salt
¼ teaspoon garlic powder
¼ teaspoon pepper
¼ teaspoon dried basil leaves
¼ teaspoon dried thyme leaves
1 bay leaf
⅛ teaspoon cayenne
1 pound fresh medium shrimp,
    peeled and deveined
    Hot cooked rice

Heat Crisco Oil in large saucepan. Add
flour. Stir until smooth. Cook over
moderate heat, stirring constantly, 3 to
4 minutes, or until lightly browned.
Add onion, celery and green pepper.
Cook over moderate heat 2 to 3
minutes, or until tender. Add remaining
ingredients except shrimp and rice.
Cover. Reduce heat. Simmer about 45
minutes, or until flavors are blended.
Stir in shrimp. Re-cover. Cook about 3
minutes longer, or until shrimp are
opaque and firm. Remove and discard
lemon slice and bay leaf. Serve
with rice.

4 to 6 servings

Beer Batter Shrimp

½ cup beer
⅓ cup all-purpose flour
⅓ cup cornstarch
1 egg
2 tablespoons Crisco Oil
⅛ teaspoon cayenne
⅛ teaspoon garlic powder
   Crisco Oil for frying
1 pound fresh medium shrimp,
   peeled, deveined and butterflied,
   page 20

Combine beer, flour, cornstarch, egg,
2 tablespoons Crisco Oil, cayenne and
garlic powder in medium mixing bowl.
Mix well. Cover and refrigerate at least
1 hour.

Heat 2 to 3 inches Crisco Oil in deep-
fryer or large saucepan to 375°F. Dip
shrimp in batter. Fry a few shrimp at a
time, 1 to 1½ minutes, or until golden
brown. Drain on paper towels. Serve
immediately or keep warm in 175°F oven.

4 to 6 servings

Deep-Fried Clams

2 cups oyster crackers, finely crushed
½ teaspoon poultry seasoning
¼ teaspoon salt
¼ teaspoon cayenne
¼ teaspoon garlic powder
¼ teaspoon ground marjoram
2 eggs, slightly beaten
1 can (10 ounces) whole baby clams,
   drained
   Crisco Oil for frying

Mix cracker crumbs, poultry seasoning,
salt, cayenne, garlic powder and
marjoram in large plastic food storage
bag. Set aside. Place eggs in small
mixing bowl. Gently stir in clams.
Remove a few clams with slotted spoon
and add to cracker mixture. Shake to
coat. Remove clams from cracker
mixture; set aside. Repeat with
remaining clams.

Heat 2 to 3 inches Crisco Oil in deep-
fryer or large saucepan to 375°F. Fry a
few clams at a time, about 30 seconds,
or until golden brown. Drain on paper
towels. Serve immediately.

2 to 4 servings

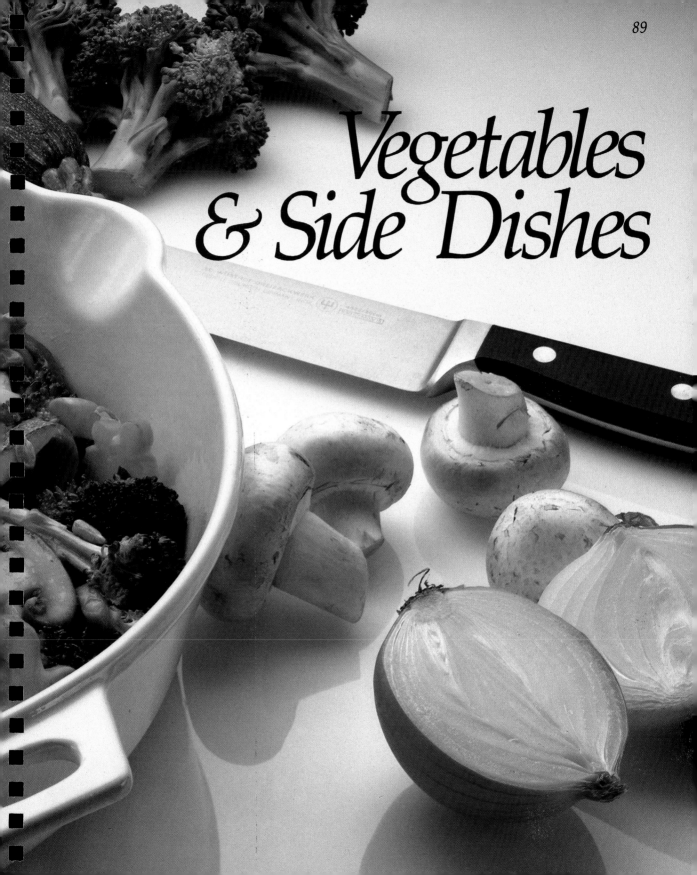

Vegetables & Side Dishes

Asparagus in Anchovy Sauce ▲

¾ cup water
¾ teaspoon salt, divided
2 packages (8 to 10 ounces each) frozen asparagus spears
1 cup Crisco Oil
3 tablespoons lemon juice
1 tablespoon anchovy paste
1 teaspoon onion powder
1 teaspoon dried chervil leaves
¼ teaspoon garlic powder

Combine water and ½ teaspoon salt in large saucepan. Heat to boiling. Add asparagus. Return to boiling. Cover. Reduce heat to moderate. Cook 3 to 4 minutes, or until asparagus is thawed and warm. Drain. Spread asparagus in shallow baking dish.

Blend remaining ingredients and remaining ¼ teaspoon salt in small mixing bowl. Pour over asparagus. Cover and refrigerate 3 to 4 hours, stirring periodically. Serve chilled or at room temperature.

4 to 6 servings

Zesty Green Beans ▲

1 cup water
1½ teaspoons salt
⅛ to ¼ teaspoon dried crushed red pepper
1½ pounds fresh green beans, trimmed and cut into 1-inch pieces
3 tablespoons Crisco Oil
1 small onion, thinly sliced

Combine water, salt and red pepper in large saucepan. Heat to boiling. Add green beans. Return to boiling. Cover. Reduce heat to moderate. Cook 10 to 15 minutes, or until tender-crisp. Drain.

Meanwhile, heat Crisco Oil in large skillet. Add onion. Sauté over moderate heat until tender. Stir in green beans. Cover. Cook 1 to 2 minutes, or until heated through.

6 servings

Cheesy Deep-Fried Broccoli ▼

4 cups water
¾ teaspoon salt, divided
3 cups fresh broccoli flowerets
¾ cup all-purpose flour, divided
4 tablespoons Grated American
   Cheese Food, divided
¼ teaspoon onion powder
1 cup buttermilk
½ teaspoon baking powder
   Crisco Oil for frying

Combine water and ½ teaspoon salt in large saucepan. Heat to boiling. Add broccoli. Return to boiling. Boil 3 minutes. Drain and rinse in cold water.

Mix ¼ cup flour, 2 tablespoons cheese and onion powder in large plastic food storage bag. Add broccoli. Shake to coat. Set aside.

Combine buttermilk, baking powder, remaining ½ cup flour, 2 tablespoons cheese and ¼ teaspoon salt in small mixing bowl. Stir until smooth.

Heat 2 to 3 inches Crisco Oil in deep-fryer or large saucepan to 375°F. Dip a few pieces broccoli in batter. Let excess batter drip back into bowl. Fry 1 to 2 minutes, or until deep golden brown. Drain on paper towels. Serve immediately or keep warm in 175°F oven. Repeat with remaining broccoli.

4 to 6 servings

Sesame Broccoli

1 cup water
½ teaspoon salt
1 pound broccoli, trimmed and cut
   into spears
4 teaspoons Crisco Oil, divided
1 tablespoon sesame seed
1 tablespoon lemon juice
1 tablespoon soy sauce
1 tablespoon sugar

Combine water and salt in large saucepan. Heat to boiling. Add broccoli. Return to boiling. Cover. Reduce heat to moderate. Cook about 10 minutes, or until tender-crisp. Drain.

Meanwhile, heat 1 teaspoon Crisco Oil in small saucepan. Add sesame seed. Cook over moderate heat, stirring constantly, until light brown. Add remaining 3 teaspoons Crisco Oil, lemon juice, soy sauce and sugar. Heat to boiling. Drizzle over broccoli.

4 to 6 servings

Brussels Sprouts Amandine ▼

1 tablespoon Crisco Oil
¼ cup sliced almonds
¾ cup water
1½ teaspoons instant beef bouillon
   granules
1 package (16 ounces) frozen Brussels
   sprouts
   Dash pepper

Heat Crisco Oil in medium saucepan. Add almonds. Sauté over moderate heat until light golden brown. Drain on paper towels.

Combine water and bouillon granules in medium saucepan. Heat to boiling. Add Brussels sprouts. Return to boiling. Cover. Reduce heat. Simmer, stirring once to break apart Brussels sprouts, 8 to 12 minutes, or until tender. Drain. Stir in almonds and pepper.

4 to 6 servings

Cabbage Cakes

2 eggs, slightly beaten
½ cup all-purpose flour
1¼ teaspoons salt, divided
½ cup milk
½ cup club soda
3 tablespoons Crisco Oil
3 cups finely-shredded cabbage
1 teaspoon sugar
¼ teaspoon pepper

Combine eggs, flour and ¼ teaspoon salt in medium mixing bowl. Stir until smooth. Blend in milk and club soda. Set aside.

Heat Crisco Oil in large skillet. Add cabbage. Sprinkle with remaining 1 teaspoon salt, sugar and pepper. Cook over moderate heat, stirring constantly, until tender. Cool slightly. Stir into batter.

Lightly oil 6-inch skillet with Crisco Oil. Heat skillet. Pour ¼ cup batter in center of skillet. Cook over moderate heat, about 2 minutes, or until light brown, turning over once. Drain on paper towels. Serve immediately or keep warm in 175°F oven. Repeat with remaining batter. Garnish with *fresh parsley sprigs*, if desired.

8 pancakes

Spiced Red Cabbage ▼

¼ cup Crisco Oil
2-pound head red cabbage, chopped
1 small onion, thinly sliced and separated into rings
1 small apple, cored and chopped
½ cup raisins
¼ teaspoon ground cloves
⅛ teaspoon ground allspice
1 tablespoon white wine vinegar
2 teaspoons sugar
1 teaspoon salt

Heat Crisco Oil in Dutch oven or large saucepan. Add cabbage, onion, apple, raisins, cloves and allspice. Stir to coat. Cover. Cook over moderate heat, stirring occasionally, about 1 hour, or until cabbage is tender. Stir in vinegar, sugar and salt.

6 to 8 servings

Carrot Nut Pudding

1 pound carrots, grated
1½ cups milk
½ teaspoon salt
½ cup whipping cream
1 tablespoon all-purpose flour
1 cup ground blanched almonds
½ cup firmly packed brown sugar
¼ cup Crisco Oil
¼ cup raisins
½ teaspoon ground turmeric
¼ teaspoon ground nutmeg

Combine carrots, milk and salt in medium saucepan. Blend cream and flour in small mixing bowl. Stir into carrot mixture. Heat to boiling, stirring constantly. Cook, uncovered, over moderate heat, stirring frequently, 40 to 45 minutes, or until liquid cooks away. Stir in remaining ingredients. Cook over low heat, stirring frequently, 10 minutes. Garnish with *slivered almonds*, if desired.

6 servings

Corn Fritters ▼

1 can (16 ounces) whole kernel corn, drained
1 cup all-purpose flour
1 cup dairy sour cream
2 eggs
2 tablespoons Crisco Oil
2 tablespoons finely-chopped onion
1 teaspoon baking powder
1 teaspoon sugar
½ teaspoon salt
¼ teaspoon ground nutmeg
⅛ teaspoon white pepper
  Crisco Oil for frying

Combine all ingredients except Crisco Oil for frying in medium mixing bowl. Mix well. Let stand 1 hour.

Heat 2 to 3 inches Crisco Oil in deep-fryer or large saucepan to 350°F. Drop batter by heaping tablespoonfuls into hot Crisco Oil. Fry a few at a time 5 to 6 minutes, or until deep golden brown. Drain on paper towels. Repeat with remaining batter. Serve immediately or keep warm in 175°F oven.

14 to 16 fritters

Cauliflower Au Gratin

1 recipe Sesame Vegetable Topping, page 101
1 cup water
¾ teaspoon salt, divided
2 packages (10 ounces each) frozen cauliflower
1 medium tomato, peeled, seeded and chopped
1 teaspoon dried parsley flakes
2 tablespoons Crisco Oil
2 tablespoons all-purpose flour
⅛ teaspoon pepper
1 cup milk
1 cup shredded Cheddar cheese (about 4 ounces)

Prepare Sesame Vegetable Topping as directed. Set aside.

Preheat oven to 350°F. Combine water and ½ teaspoon salt in large saucepan. Heat to boiling. Add cauliflower. Return to boiling. Cover. Reduce heat to moderate. Cook 3 minutes, or until cauliflower is thawed and warm. Drain. Place in 2-quart casserole. Stir in tomato and parsley flakes. Set aside.

Blend Crisco Oil, flour, remaining ¼ teaspoon salt and pepper in small saucepan. Slowly stir in milk. Cook over moderate heat, stirring constantly, until thickened and bubbly. Add cheese. Stir until cheese melts. Pour over cauliflower mixture. Sprinkle with Sesame Vegetable Topping. Bake at 350°F, 25 to 30 minutes, or until bubbly.

6 to 8 servings

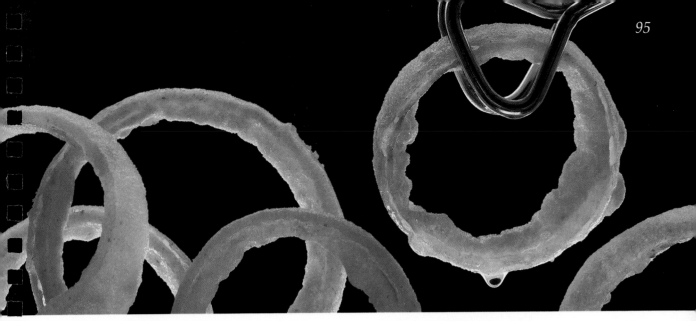

Fried Eggplant

1 cup unseasoned dry bread crumbs
¼ cup grated Parmesan cheese
1 teaspoon Italian seasoning
½ teaspoon salt
½ cup all-purpose flour
2 eggs
¼ cup milk
1 pound eggplant, peeled and cut into
    ¼-inch slices
    Crisco Oil for frying

Mix bread crumbs, Parmesan cheese, Italian seasoning and salt in shallow dish. Place flour on sheet of waxed paper. Blend eggs and milk in another shallow dish. Dip each slice of eggplant first in flour, then in egg mixture, then in bread crumb mixture to coat.

Heat ¼ inch Crisco Oil in medium skillet. Fry a few slices eggplant at a time over moderate heat 4 to 5 minutes, or until golden brown, turning over once. Drain on paper towels. Serve immediately or keep warm in 175°F oven. Garnish with *grated Parmesan cheese*, if desired.

4 to 6 servings

Onion Rings ▲

Batter:
¾ cup all-purpose flour
½ cup water
½ cup milk
6 tablespoons white cornmeal
1 tablespoon Crisco Oil
¾ teaspoon seasoned salt
½ teaspoon sugar
5 or 6 drops hot red pepper sauce

    Crisco Oil for frying
1 large onion, cut into ½-inch slices
    and separated into rings

For batter, combine all ingredients in small mixing bowl. Stir until smooth.

Heat 2 to 3 inches Crisco Oil in deep-fryer or large saucepan to 375°F. Dip a few onion rings in batter. Let excess batter drip back into bowl. Fry a few at a time 2 to 3 minutes, or until golden brown. Drain on paper towels. Repeat with remaining onion. Serve immediately or keep warm in 175°F oven.

4 to 6 servings

French Green Peas ▼

> 4 slices bacon, cooked and crumbled with 2 tablespoons drippings reserved
> 2 tablespoons Crisco Oil
> ¼ cup all-purpose flour
> 2½ cups chicken broth
> 2 packages (10 ounces each) frozen green peas
> 2 small onions, thinly sliced
> 2 teaspoons dried parsley flakes
> ½ teaspoon salt
> ⅛ teaspoon pepper

Combine reserved bacon drippings and Crisco Oil in large saucepan. Stir in flour. Cook over moderate heat, stirring constantly, 3 to 4 minutes, or until light brown. Gradually stir in broth. Heat to boiling. Add peas, onions, parsley flakes, salt and pepper. Return to boiling. Cover. Reduce heat. Simmer, stirring occasionally to break apart peas, 20 minutes, or until onion is tender. Sprinkle with crumbled bacon. Garnish with *sliced pimiento*, if desired.

8 servings

Potato Pancakes

> 4 medium white potatoes, peeled and coarsely shredded
> 1 small onion, grated
> 1 egg
> ⅓ cup all-purpose flour
> 1½ teaspoons salt
> ⅛ teaspoon pepper
> 2 tablespoons Crisco Oil

Combine potatoes, onion, egg, flour, salt and pepper in medium mixing bowl. Mix well. Heat Crisco Oil in large skillet. Spoon ¼ cup potato mixture into skillet for each of 4 pancakes. Flatten with spatula. Cook over moderate heat 10 to 15 minutes, or until golden brown, turning over once. Drain on paper towels. Add additional Crisco Oil, if necessary. Repeat with remaining potato mixture.

6 to 8 servings

NOTE: To keep shredded potatoes from turning brown, place in cold water until ready to use. Drain thoroughly and pat dry between paper towels before using.

Fried Potato Wedges

> 4 medium white potatoes, baked
> Crisco Oil for frying

Cut each potato into 6 wedges. Heat 2 to 3 inches Crisco Oil in deep-fryer or large saucepan to 375°F. Fry half the wedges at a time 2 to 3 minutes, or until golden brown. Drain on paper towels. Serve immediately.

4 to 6 servings

Fried Rice ▼

4 tablespoons Crisco Oil, divided
¼ cup chopped green onion
¼ cup chopped carrot
2 eggs, slightly beaten
2 tablespoons soy sauce
1 tablespoon white wine
2 teaspoons sugar
¼ teaspoon garlic powder
⅛ teaspoon cayenne (optional)
3 cups cooked long grain rice
2 cups fresh bean sprouts
1 cup frozen green peas, thawed
1 can (8 ounces) sliced water
    chestnuts, drained
½ cup sliced fresh mushrooms

Heat 2 tablespoons Crisco Oil in large skillet. Add onion and carrot. Sauté over moderate heat until tender. Stir in eggs. Cook, stirring constantly, until set but moist. Remove egg mixture from skillet; set aside.

Combine remaining 2 tablespoons Crisco Oil, soy sauce, wine, sugar, garlic powder and cayenne (optional) in small bowl. Mix rice, bean sprouts, peas, water chestnuts and mushrooms in large skillet. Add soy sauce mixture. Cook over moderate heat, stirring occasionally, 5 to 8 minutes, or until mushrooms are tender. Stir in egg mixture.

6 servings

Spicy Rice

2 tablespoons Crisco Oil
1 cup uncooked long grain rice
1 small onion, halved lengthwise
    and thinly sliced
2 cups water
2 tablespoons raisins
1 teaspoon salt
3 whole cloves
1 bay leaf
⅛ teaspoon ground cardamom
⅛ teaspoon pepper

Heat Crisco Oil in large saucepan. Add rice and onion. Cook over moderate heat, stirring constantly, until golden brown. Add remaining ingredients. Heat to boiling. Cover. Reduce heat. Simmer 20 to 25 minutes, or until rice is tender. Remove and discard cloves and bay leaf.

6 servings

Chinese Spinach ▲

3 tablespoons Crisco Oil
1 tablespoon soy sauce
1 teaspoon lime juice
½ teaspoon sugar
⅛ teaspoon pepper
1 clove garlic, minced
½ cup diagonally-sliced green onion, 1-inch slices
12 ounces fresh spinach, trimmed, washed and torn into bite-size pieces
¼ cup sliced water chestnuts
1 jar (2 ounces) sliced pimiento, drained

Heat Crisco Oil, soy sauce, lime juice, sugar and pepper in large skillet. Add garlic. Stir-fry over medium-high heat about 1 minute, or until garlic is light brown. Add onion. Stir-fry 1 minute. Add spinach, water chestnuts and pimiento. Stir-fry 2 to 3 minutes longer, or until spinach is tender.

4 to 6 servings

Spinach Almond Casserole

1 recipe Sesame Vegetable Topping, page 101
2 packages (10 ounces each) frozen chopped spinach, thawed
2 tablespoons Crisco Oil
¼ cup chopped onion
2 tablespoons chopped celery
2 tablespoons all-purpose flour
1 teaspoon salt
½ teaspoon dried dill weed
⅛ teaspoon pepper
1 cup half-and-half
1 egg, slightly beaten
3 tablespoons chopped almonds

Prepare Sesame Vegetable Topping as directed. Set aside.

Preheat oven to 325°F. Lightly oil 1-quart casserole with Crisco Oil. Set aside.

Press excess moisture from spinach. Set aside.

Heat Crisco Oil in medium saucepan. Add onion and celery. Sauté over moderate heat until tender. Remove from heat. Stir in flour, salt, dill weed and pepper. Return to heat. Blend in half-and-half. Cook, stirring constantly, until bubbly. Remove from heat. Blend in egg. Stir in spinach and almonds. Transfer to prepared casserole. Sprinkle with Sesame Vegetable Topping. Bake at 325°F, 35 to 40 minutes, or until hot and topping is light brown.

6 to 8 servings

Savory Sausage Dressing ▼

1 package (12 ounces) seasoned bulk
  pork sausage
¼ cup Crisco Oil
½ cup chopped onion
½ cup chopped celery
1 clove garlic, minced
1½ cups sliced fresh mushrooms
½ teaspoon Worcestershire sauce
¼ teaspoon dried rosemary leaves
⅛ teaspoon pepper
2 cups herb-seasoned stuffing mix
1 egg, slightly beaten
½ cup hot water
1½ teaspoons instant chicken bouillon
  granules

Preheat oven to 325°F. Place sausage in large skillet. Cook over medium-high heat until no longer pink. Drain. Transfer to medium mixing bowl.

Heat Crisco Oil in large skillet. Add onion, celery and garlic. Sauté over moderate heat until celery is tender-crisp. Add mushrooms, Worcestershire sauce, rosemary and pepper. Cook, stirring constantly, 1 minute. Add to sausage. Mix well. Stir in stuffing mix and egg. Mix hot water and bouillon granules in small bowl. Stir into stuffing mixture. Place in 1½-quart casserole. Bake at 325°F, 30 to 35 minutes, or until heated through.

6 to 8 servings

Stuffed Tomatoes

6 to 8 medium tomatoes
2 tablespoons Crisco Oil
⅓ cup chopped celery
2 tablespoons chopped onion
2 cups cooked brown rice
¼ cup grated Parmesan cheese
1 tablespoon snipped fresh parsley
1 teaspoon dried basil leaves
⅛ teaspoon pepper
⅛ teaspoon garlic powder

Cut thin slice from top of each tomato. Set aside. Scoop out center of tomatoes; chop pulp and set aside. Place shells upside-down on paper towels to drain.

Preheat oven to 350°F. Heat Crisco Oil in medium saucepan. Add celery and onion. Sauté over moderate heat until celery is tender. Remove from heat. Add reserved tomato pulp, rice, Parmesan cheese, parsley, basil, pepper and garlic powder. Mix well. Fill each tomato shell with one-fourth rice mixture. Replace tomato tops, if desired.

Lightly oil 9-inch pie plate or round baking dish with Crisco Oil. Place tomatoes in dish. Cover with aluminum foil. Bake at 350°F, 30 to 45 minutes, or until tomatoes are tender.

6 to 8 servings

NOTE: Use 1 lightly-oiled custard cup for each tomato instead of pie plate or baking dish, if desired.

Italian Vegetable Sauté ▼

2 tablespoons Crisco Oil
1 clove garlic, minced
¼ teaspoon dried oregano leaves
¼ teaspoon dried marjoram leaves
2 cups julienne-cut zucchini
1 small onion, thinly sliced and separated into rings
1 can (16 ounces) whole tomatoes, drained, cut up
2 tablespoons sliced pitted black olives (optional)
½ teaspoon salt
⅛ teaspoon pepper
2 tablespoons grated Parmesan cheese

Heat Crisco Oil in large skillet. Add garlic, oregano and marjoram. Sauté over moderate heat until garlic is light brown. Add zucchini and onion. Stir to coat. Sauté 5 to 7 minutes, or until tender. Stir in tomatoes, olives (optional), salt and pepper. Cook until heated through. Stir in Parmesan cheese.

4 to 6 servings

Nutty Vegetable Stir-Fry*

¾ to 1 pound fresh broccoli
¼ cup Crisco Oil
1 medium zucchini, cut into julienne
   strips
1 small onion, halved lengthwise
   and thinly sliced
⅛ teaspoon dried crushed red pepper
1 cup sliced fresh mushrooms
2 tablespoons sunflower nuts
2 teaspoons soy sauce

Trim and discard tough ends from broccoli stalk. Cut stalk into thin slices. Separate head into flowerets.

Heat Crisco Oil in large skillet. Add broccoli, zucchini, onion and red pepper. Stir-fry over medium-high heat about 5 minutes, or until broccoli is tender-crisp. Add mushrooms. Stir-fry 1 minute longer, or until mushrooms are tender. Stir in sunflower nuts and soy sauce.

4 to 6 servings

*Pictured on pages 88-89.

Sesame Vegetable Topping

2 tablespoons Crisco Oil
2 tablespoons finely-chopped onion
2 teaspoons sesame seed
½ cup buttery round cracker crumbs

Heat Crisco Oil in small skillet. Add onion. Sauté over moderate heat until tender-crisp. Add sesame seed. Cook, stirring constantly, 1 minute. Remove from heat. Stir in cracker crumbs. Use as a topping for vegetable dishes.

About ½ cup

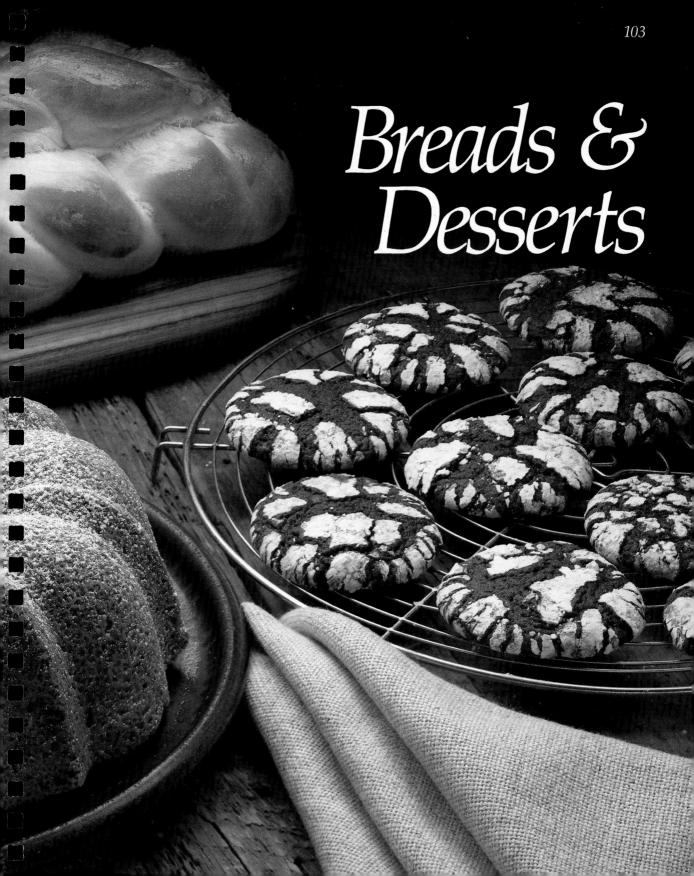

Breads & Desserts

Double-Braided Saffron Bread ▼

4½ to 5½ cups unsifted all-purpose
    flour, divided
  2 tablespoons sugar
  1 package (¼ ounce) active dry yeast
1½ teaspoons salt
  ⅓ cup Crisco Oil
  1 cup very warm water (120° to 130°F)
  ⅛ teaspoon powdered saffron
  4 eggs
  1 teaspoon cold water

Mix 1¼ cups flour, sugar, yeast and salt in large mixing bowl. Stir in Crisco Oil. Combine warm water and saffron in small bowl. Stir until saffron is dissolved. Add to flour mixture. Beat at medium speed of electric mixer 3 minutes, scraping bowl occasionally. Separate 1 egg; set yolk aside. Add egg white to flour mixture. Add remaining 3 eggs and ½ cup flour. Beat at medium speed 1 minute, scraping bowl occasionally. Stir in enough remaining flour to make soft dough.

Knead dough on lightly-floured surface 8 to 10 minutes, or until smooth and elastic, adding additional flour as necessary. Place in lightly-oiled large mixing bowl. Turn dough over to coat both sides with Crisco Oil. Cover; let rise in warm place 1 to 1½ hours, or until doubled.

Oil baking sheet. Set aside. Punch down dough. Place on lightly-floured surface. Set aside two-thirds of dough. Divide remaining dough into 6 equal portions. Roll each portion with floured fingers into a 10-inch long piece. Braid 3 pieces together. Braid remaining 3 pieces. Set aside.

Divide remaining dough into 6 equal portions. Roll each portion with floured fingers into a 12-inch long piece. Braid 3 pieces together. Braid remaining 3 pieces. For each loaf, center 1 small braid on top of 1 large braid. Press ends together to seal. Place both loaves on prepared baking sheet.

Blend reserved egg yolk and cold water in small bowl. Brush on both loaves. Cover; let rise in warm place about 1 hour, or until doubled. Preheat oven to 400°F. Bake loaves at 400°F, 20 to 25 minutes, or until loaves are golden brown and sound hollow when tapped lightly. Cool on wire rack.

2 loaves

How to Braid Saffron Loaves

Divide one-third of dough into 6 equal portions. With floured fingers, roll each portion into a 10-inch long piece. Braid 3 pieces. Braid remaining 3 pieces.

Divide remaining dough into 6 equal portions. Roll each portion into a 12-inch long piece and make into 2 braids, using 3 pieces for each braid.

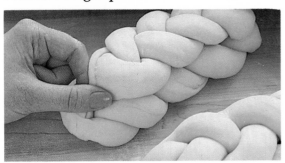

Center 1 small braid on top of 1 large braid for each loaf. Press ends together to seal. Let rise and bake as directed.

Beer Cheese Bread ▼

1½ cups unsifted all-purpose flour
 ½ cup whole wheat flour
 2 tablespoons sugar
1½ teaspoons baking powder
 1 teaspoon instant minced onion
 ¾ teaspoon baking soda
 ½ teaspoon salt
 2 cups shredded Cheddar cheese
    (about 8 ounces)
 1 cup beer
 2 eggs
 ⅓ cup Crisco Oil

Preheat oven to 350°F. Oil and flour 9 × 5-inch loaf pan. Set aside.

Mix all-purpose flour, whole wheat flour, sugar, baking powder, onion, baking soda and salt in medium mixing bowl. Add remaining ingredients. Beat at medium speed of electric mixer about 1 minute, scraping bowl occasionally. Pour into prepared pan.

Bake at 350°F, 50 to 60 minutes, or until golden brown and wooden pick inserted in center comes out clean. Immediately remove from pan. Cool on wire rack.

1 loaf

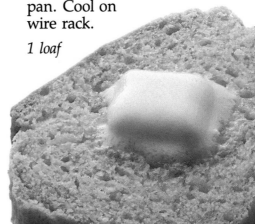

Soda Bread

- 3 cups unsifted all-purpose flour
- 3 tablespoons sugar
- 2 teaspoons baking powder
- 1 teaspoon baking soda
- 1 teaspoon salt
- 1½ cups buttermilk
- 1 egg, slightly beaten
- 3 tablespoons Crisco Oil
- ½ cup raisins

Preheat oven to 350°F. Oil 8-inch round baking dish. Set aside.

Mix flour, sugar, baking powder, baking soda and salt in medium mixing bowl. Add buttermilk, egg and Crisco Oil. Stir with fork until ingredients are moistened. Stir in raisins. Pour into prepared dish.

Bake at 350°F, 35 to 40 minutes, or until golden brown and wooden pick inserted in center comes out clean. Cool 10 minutes. Remove from dish. Cool completely on wire rack.

One 8-inch round loaf

Mexican Cornbread ▼

- 1 cup yellow cornmeal
- ⅔ cup unsifted all-purpose flour
- 2 teaspoons baking powder
- ½ teaspoon salt
- ¾ cup dairy sour cream
- 2 eggs
- ¼ cup Crisco Oil
- 2 cups shredded Cheddar cheese (about 8 ounces), divided
- 1 can (8¾ ounces) whole kernel corn, drained
- 1 can (4 ounces) chopped green chilies, drained

Preheat oven to 350°F. Oil 8-inch square baking pan. Set aside.

Mix cornmeal, flour, baking powder and salt in small mixing bowl. Set aside. Blend sour cream, eggs and Crisco Oil in medium mixing bowl. Add cornmeal mixture, 1½ cups Cheddar cheese, corn and chilies. Mix well. Pour into prepared pan. Sprinkle with remaining ½ cup Cheddar cheese. Bake at 350°F, 30 to 35 minutes, or until wooden pick inserted in center comes out clean. Cut into squares and serve warm.

*One 8-inch
square pan*

Molasses Muffins ▼

1⅔ cups unsifted all-purpose flour
3 tablespoons sugar
2 teaspoons baking powder
1 teaspoon ground ginger
½ teaspoon salt
½ cup dark molasses
2 eggs, slightly beaten
¼ cup Crisco Oil
¼ cup milk

Preheat oven to 400°F. Place paper liners in 12 muffin cups. Set aside.

Mix flour, sugar, baking powder, ginger and salt in medium mixing bowl. Make a well in center of mixture. Set aside. Blend remaining ingredients in small mixing bowl. Pour into well in dry ingredients. Stir just until ingredients are moistened. Pour into lined muffin cups, filling each about ⅔ full. Bake at 400°F, about 15 minutes, or until centers spring back when touched lightly.

Orange Raisin Muffins: Follow recipe above, omitting ginger. Add ½ cup raisins and 2 teaspoons grated orange peel to dry ingredients.

1 dozen muffins

Old-Fashioned Apple Loaf

2 cups unsifted all-purpose flour
2 teaspoons baking powder
1 teaspoon apple pie spice*
½ teaspoon salt
¼ teaspoon baking soda
⅔ cup chunky apple sauce
½ cup granulated sugar
2 eggs
¼ cup Crisco Oil
2 tablespoons milk
2 tablespoons chopped walnuts
2 teaspoons butter or margarine
1 teaspoon packed brown sugar

Preheat oven to 350°F. Oil and flour 8 × 4-inch loaf pan. Set aside.

Mix flour, baking powder, apple pie spice, salt and baking soda in medium mixing bowl. Set aside. Combine apple sauce, granulated sugar, eggs, Crisco Oil and milk in large mixing bowl. Mix well. Add dry ingredients. Beat at medium speed of electric mixer just until combined, scraping bowl occasionally. Pour into prepared pan.

Combine walnuts, butter and brown sugar in small mixing bowl. Mix with fork until crumbly. Sprinkle down center of loaf. Bake at 350°F, 35 to 45 minutes, or until golden brown and wooden pick inserted in center comes out clean. Immediately remove from pan. Cool on wire rack.

*Substitute ¾ teaspoon ground cinnamon, dash ground nutmeg and dash ground cloves for apple pie spice if desired.

1 loaf

Italian Pepperoni Puffs ▼

2¼ to 2¾ cups unsifted all-purpose
    flour, divided
1 package (¼ ounce) active dry yeast
1 tablespoon sugar
1 teaspoon garlic salt
½ teaspoon Italian seasoning
¼ teaspoon onion powder
¾ cup very warm water (120° to 130°F)
2 tablespoons Crisco Oil
1 egg
½ cup grated Parmesan cheese
¼ cup finely-chopped pepperoni
    Crisco Oil for frying

Mix 1½ cups flour, yeast, sugar, garlic salt, Italian seasoning and onion powder in large mixing bowl. Add warm water, Crisco Oil and egg. Beat at low speed of electric mixer until ingredients are moistened, scraping bowl constantly. Beat at medium speed 3 minutes, scraping bowl occasionally. Stir in Parmesan cheese and enough remaining flour to make a slightly stiff dough.

Knead dough on lightly-floured surface 5 to 8 minutes, or until smooth and elastic, adding additional flour as necessary. Place in lightly-oiled medium mixing bowl. Turn dough over to coat both sides with Crisco Oil. Cover; let rise in warm place 40 to 50 minutes, or until doubled.

Punch down dough. Place on lightly-floured surface. Divide dough in half. Roll each half to ⅛-inch thickness. Cut into 2-inch rounds. Place ½ teaspoon chopped pepperoni in center of half of rounds. Brush edges with water. Top with remaining rounds. Press edges together with fork to seal. Cover; let rise in warm place about 30 minutes, or until doubled.

Heat 2 to 3 inches Crisco Oil in deep-fryer or large saucepan to 365°F. Fry 3 to 4 puffs at a time, 3 to 4 minutes, or until golden brown, turning over several times. Drain on paper towels. Sprinkle with *grated Parmesan cheese*, if desired. Serve warm.

1½ to 2 dozen puffs

Raised Doughnuts ▲

3½ to 4½ cups unsifted all-purpose
    flour, divided
¾ cup sugar, divided
2 packages (¼ ounce each) active dry
    yeast
1 teaspoon salt
1 cup milk
¼ cup vegetable shortening
2 eggs, slightly beaten
    Crisco Oil for frying

Mix 2 cups flour, ¼ cup sugar, yeast
and salt in large mixing bowl. Set aside.
Combine milk and shortening in small
saucepan. Cook over moderate heat
until very warm (120° to 130°F). Add to
flour mixture. Add eggs. Beat at low
speed of electric mixer 1 minute,
scraping bowl constantly. Beat at
medium speed 3 minutes, scraping
bowl occasionally. Stir in enough
remaining flour to make a soft dough.

Knead dough on lightly-floured surface
5 to 8 minutes, or until smooth and
elastic, adding additional flour as
necessary (dough will be slightly
sticky). Place in lightly-oiled medium
mixing bowl. Turn dough over to coat
both sides with Crisco Oil. Cover; let
rise in warm place 40 to 50 minutes, or
until doubled.

Oil baking sheet. Set aside. Punch
down dough. Place on lightly-floured
surface. Divide dough in half. Roll each
half to ½-inch thickness. Cut into
2½-inch rounds with doughnut cutter.
Place doughnuts and holes on prepared
baking sheet. Cover; let rise in warm
place about 30 minutes, or until doubled.

Heat 2 to 3 inches Crisco Oil in
deep-fryer or large saucepan to 375°F.
Fry 2 or 3 doughnuts at a time, 1 to 1½
minutes, or until golden brown, turning
over once. To fry holes, place several at
a time in hot Crisco Oil. Fry 45 to 60
seconds, or until golden brown, turning
over occasionally. Drain on paper
towels. Place remaining ½ cup sugar in
large plastic food storage bag. Add a
few doughnuts and holes at a time;
shake to coat.

Glazed Raised Doughnuts: Follow recipe
above, except reduce sugar to ¼ cup
and do not shake doughnuts in sugar.
Before frying doughnuts, combine 1 cup
confectioners sugar, 2 tablespoons milk,
1 tablespoon honey and 1 teaspoon
grated lemon or orange peel in small
mixing bowl. Beat at medium speed of
electric mixer until smooth. After frying,
dip one side of warm doughnuts in
glaze. Cool doughnuts, glazed-side up,
on wire rack over waxed paper.

1½ dozen doughnuts and 1½ dozen holes

◀ French Breakfast Puffs

1½ cups unsifted all-purpose flour
½ cup confectioners sugar
1 teaspoon baking powder
1 teaspoon salt
¾ teaspoon ground nutmeg
½ cup milk
½ cup water
¼ cup Crisco Oil
1½ teaspoons grated lemon peel
3 eggs
Crisco Oil for frying
Confectioners sugar

Mix flour, ½ cup confectioners sugar, baking powder, salt and nutmeg in small mixing bowl. Set aside. Combine milk, water, Crisco Oil and lemon peel in medium saucepan. Heat to rolling boil over medium-high heat. Add flour mixture all at once. Beat with wooden spoon until mixture pulls away from sides of pan into a ball. Remove from heat; cool slightly. Add eggs, one at a time, beating after each addition.

Heat 2 to 3 inches Crisco Oil in deep-fryer or large saucepan to 350°F.

Drop dough by tablespoonfuls into hot Crisco Oil. Fry 3 or 4 puffs at a time, 4 to 6 minutes, or until golden brown, turning over several times. Drain on paper towels. Sprinkle top of each puff with confectioners sugar.

32 puffs

Southern Hush Puppies ▶

Crisco Oil for frying
¾ cup yellow cornmeal
⅓ cup unsifted all-purpose flour
1½ teaspoons baking powder
½ teaspoon salt
½ cup buttermilk
1 egg
¼ cup finely-chopped onion

Heat 2 to 3 inches Crisco Oil in deep-fryer or large saucepan to 375°F. Meanwhile, mix cornmeal, flour, baking powder and salt in medium mixing bowl. Add remaining ingredients. Mix well. Drop batter by tablespoonfuls into hot Crisco Oil. Fry a few at a time, 3 to 4 minutes, or until golden brown. Drain on paper towels. Serve immediately or keep warm in 175°F oven. Repeat with remaining batter.

About 1 dozen hush puppies

Crunchy Peaches with Melba Sauce

1 package (10 ounces) frozen sweetened raspberries, thawed
1 tablespoon orange-flavored liqueur
2 cans (16 ounces each) peach halves, drained
3 cups cornflake cereal, finely crushed
1 tablespoon unsifted all-purpose flour
1 teaspoon ground cinnamon
1 egg
Crisco Oil for frying

Combine raspberries and liqueur in blender pitcher. Blend until smooth. Set sauce aside.

Place peach halves on paper towels to drain. Combine crushed cereal, flour and cinnamon in shallow dish or on sheet of waxed paper. Place egg in another shallow dish; beat slightly. Dip each peach half in egg, then in cereal crumb mixture, pressing to coat thoroughly.

Heat 2 to 3 inches Crisco Oil in deep-fryer or large saucepan to 350°F. Fry a few peaches at a time, about 1 minute, or until golden brown, turning over once. Drain on paper towels. Serve warm with sauce.

4 to 6 servings

Crepes

- **¾ cup unsifted all-purpose flour**
- **2 tablespoons confectioners sugar**
- **¼ teaspoon salt**
- **¾ cup milk**
- **2 eggs, slightly beaten**
- **2 tablespoons Crisco Oil**

Mix flour, sugar and salt in small mixing bowl. Add milk, eggs and Crisco Oil, stirring until smooth. Cover and refrigerate 1 hour.

Lightly oil 6-inch skillet with a non-stick surface. Heat skillet. Add 2 tablespoons batter, tilting skillet to make 6-inch crepe. Cook over moderate heat 30 to 60 seconds, or until bottom is light brown. Turn crepe over. Cook 30 to 45 seconds longer, or until bottom is light brown. Cool on wire rack. Lightly oil skillet, if necessary. Repeat with remaining batter.

Twelve 6-inch crepes

NOTE: To store crepes up to 2 days, layer between sheets of waxed paper. Wrap in plastic wrap and refrigerate.

Fruit Crepes

- **1 recipe Crepes, left**
- **1 cup plain yogurt**
- **3 tablespoons honey**
- **2 large bananas, thinly sliced**
- **1 can (11 ounces) mandarin orange sections, drained**
- **½ cup chopped maraschino cherries**

Prepare Crepes as directed. Set aside.

Blend yogurt and honey in small mixing bowl. Remove ½ cup and place in another small mixing bowl. To ½ cup mixture, stir in bananas, orange sections and cherries. Spread scant ¼ cup fruit mixture down center of each crepe. Fold opposite edges of crepe over fruit mixture. Arrange 2 crepes on each serving plate. Top crepes with remaining yogurt mixture.

6 servings

Apple Brown Betty Crepes ▼

1 recipe Crepes, page 112
6 cups thinly-sliced apples
⅔ cup firmly packed brown sugar
⅓ cup water
2 tablespoons honey
2 teaspoons lemon juice
1 teaspoon ground cinnamon
½ teaspoon salt
¼ teaspoon ground nutmeg
2 tablespoons unsifted all-purpose flour
1 tablespoon granulated sugar
1 cup chopped walnuts
2 tablespoons butter or margarine

Topping:
⅓ cup graham cracker crumbs
1 tablespoon packed brown sugar
1 tablespoon Crisco Oil

Prepare Crepes as directed. Set aside.

Mix apples, brown sugar, water, honey, lemon juice, cinnamon, salt and nutmeg in medium saucepan. Heat to boiling. Reduce heat to moderate. Cover. Cook, stirring occasionally, about 10 minutes, or until apples are tender. Mix flour and granulated sugar in small bowl. Stir into apple mixture. Cook, stirring constantly, 1 to 2 minutes longer, or until mixture thickens. Remove from heat. Add walnuts and butter, stirring until butter melts.

Preheat oven to 400°F. Lightly oil 13 × 9-inch baking pan. Spread about 2 tablespoons filling down center of each crepe. Fold opposite edges of crepe over apple mixture. Arrange crepes in prepared pan. Spread remaining apple mixture over crepes. For topping, mix all ingredients in small bowl. Sprinkle over crepes. Bake at 400°F, about 10 minutes, or until hot. Top with *whipped cream*, if desired.

6 servings

Single Pie Crust

1⅓ cups unsifted all-purpose flour
 ½ teaspoon salt
 6 tablespoons Crisco Oil
 3 tablespoons milk

Preheat oven to 375°F. Combine flour and salt in medium mixing bowl. Blend Crisco Oil and milk in small mixing bowl. Add to flour mixture. Stir with fork until mixture forms a ball. Shape into ball; flatten slightly. Place between sheets of waxed paper. Roll to a circle at least 2 inches larger than inverted 9-inch pie plate. Remove waxed paper. Fit dough into pie plate. Trim and flute edges. Prick thoroughly with fork. Bake at 375°F, 12 to 15 minutes, or until light golden brown. Cool completely.

One 9-inch pie crust

Pastry for Two-Crust Pie

2⅔ cups unsifted all-purpose flour
 1 teaspoon salt
 ¾ cup Crisco Oil
 6 tablespoons milk

Combine flour and salt in medium mixing bowl. Blend Crisco Oil and milk in small mixing bowl. Add to flour mixture. Stir with fork until mixture forms a ball. Divide dough in half; set one half aside. Shape remaining half into a ball; flatten slightly. Place between sheets of waxed paper. Roll to a circle at least 2 inches larger than inverted 9-inch pie plate. Fit dough into pie plate. Add filling. Roll out remaining dough. Place over filling. Trim and flute edges. Cut slits in top so steam can escape. Bake according to pie recipe.

Two 9-inch pie crusts

Chocolate Almond Pie

1 recipe Single Pie Crust, left
 1 package (8 ounces) cream cheese, softened
 ¼ cup chocolate syrup
 ½ teaspoon almond extract
 1 package (5⅛ or 5¼ ounces) chocolate pudding or pie filling, prepared according to package directions for pie filling
 1 tablespoon Crisco Oil
 ¼ cup sliced almonds

Prepare and bake Single Pie Crust as directed. Set aside.

Blend cream cheese, chocolate syrup and almond extract in large mixing bowl. Add prepared pie filling. Beat at medium speed of electric mixer until smooth, scraping bowl frequently. Pour into pie crust. Set aside.

Heat Crisco Oil in small skillet. Add almonds. Cook over moderate heat, stirring constantly, until almonds are golden brown. Drain on paper towels. Cool. Sprinkle onto pie. Refrigerate 2 to 3 hours, or until set.

One 9-inch pie

Peach Tart ▼

1¼ cups unsifted all-purpose flour, divided
½ teaspoon salt
¼ cup Crisco Oil
2 tablespoons plus 1½ teaspoons cold water
8 tablespoons peach preserves, divided
6 fresh peaches, peeled and sliced, or 2 cans (16 ounces each) peach slices, drained
1 teaspoon hot water

Preheat oven to 375°F. Mix 1 cup flour and salt in small mixing bowl. Set aside. Beat Crisco Oil and cold water in small mixing bowl until thickened and creamy. Immediately add to flour mixture. Stir with fork until ingredients are moistened. (If dough seems dry, add 1 to 2 tablespoons Crisco Oil.) Shape pastry into ball; flatten slightly. Place between sheets of waxed paper.

Roll to a circle at least 2 inches larger than inverted 9-inch pie plate or quiche dish. Press into pie plate. Trim and flute edges.

Mix 3 tablespoons peach preserves and remaining ¼ cup flour in small mixing bowl. Spread in bottom of pastry shell. Arrange peach slices, slightly overlapping, in pastry shell. Mix 2 tablespoons peach preserves and hot water in small bowl. Brush on peaches.

Bake at 375°F, 40 to 45 minutes, or until peaches are tender and pastry is light brown. Set on wire rack. Heat remaining 3 tablespoons peach preserves in small saucepan over moderate heat. Brush onto peaches. Cool completely.

One 9-inch tart

Carrot Cake ▲

2¼ cups unsifted all-purpose flour
1½ cups sugar
 2 teaspoons baking soda
1½ teaspoons ground cinnamon
 ½ teaspoon ground nutmeg
 ½ teaspoon salt
 1 cup Crisco Oil
 3 eggs
 ½ cup milk
 2 cups shredded carrot
1½ cups flaked coconut
 ¾ cup chopped nuts
 ½ cup currants or raisins

Frosting:
 1 package (3 ounces) cream cheese,
    softened
 2 tablespoons butter or margarine,
    softened
 2 tablespoons milk
 ¼ teaspoon vanilla
    Dash salt
 2 to 2¼ cups confectioners sugar

Preheat oven to 325°F. Oil and flour
13 × 9-inch baking pan. Set aside.

Mix flour, sugar, baking soda,
cinnamon, nutmeg and salt in large
mixing bowl. Add Crisco Oil, eggs, milk
and carrot. Beat at low speed of electric
mixer until ingredients are moistened,
scraping bowl constantly. Beat at
medium speed 2 minutes, scraping
bowl occasionally. Stir in remaining
cake ingredients. Pour into prepared
pan. Bake at 325°F, 55 to 60 minutes, or
until wooden pick inserted in center
comes out clean. Cool completely.

For frosting, blend cream cheese and
butter in small mixing bowl. Add milk,
vanilla and salt. Mix well. Stir in
enough confectioners sugar to make
desired consistency. Spread on
cooled cake.

One 13 × 9-inch cake

◄ Chocolate Yogurt Cake

2 cups unsifted all-purpose flour
1½ cups sugar
½ cup cocoa
2 teaspoons baking soda
1 teaspoon salt
1 cup plain yogurt
3 eggs
⅔ cup Crisco Oil
1½ teaspoons vanilla

Frosting:
1 package (6 ounces) semisweet chocolate chips
¼ cup butter or margarine
⅔ cup plain yogurt
½ teaspoon vanilla
⅛ teaspoon salt
2½ to 3 cups confectioners sugar

Preheat oven to 350°F. Grease and flour two 9-inch round pans. Set aside.

Mix flour, sugar, cocoa, baking soda and salt in large mixing bowl. Add yogurt, eggs, Crisco Oil and vanilla. Beat at low speed of electric mixer until ingredients are moistened, scraping bowl constantly. Beat at medium speed 2 minutes, scraping bowl occasionally. Pour into prepared pans. Bake at 350°F, 30 to 35 minutes, or until wooden pick inserted in center comes out clean. Cool 10 minutes. Remove from pans. Cool completely on wire rack.

For frosting, combine chocolate chips and butter in small saucepan. Cook over low heat, stirring constantly, until melted. Transfer mixture to medium mixing bowl. Cool slightly. Blend in yogurt, vanilla and salt. Stir in enough confectioners sugar to make desired consistency. Spread on cooled cake.

One 2-layer cake

Colonial Apple Cake*

2¾ cups unsifted all-purpose flour
1 teaspoon baking powder
1 teaspoon ground cinnamon
¾ teaspoon salt
½ teaspoon baking soda
1¾ cups granulated sugar
1¼ cups Crisco Oil
2 eggs
¼ cup milk
1 teaspoon vanilla
2 cups chopped, peeled apple
½ cup chopped dates
1 teaspoon grated lemon peel
1 to 2 tablespoons confectioners sugar

Preheat oven to 350°F. Grease and flour 12-cup fluted ring pan. Set aside.

Mix flour, baking powder, cinnamon, salt and baking soda in medium mixing bowl. Set aside. Combine granulated sugar, Crisco Oil, eggs, milk and vanilla in large mixing bowl. Beat at medium speed of electric mixer until blended, scraping bowl constantly. Add dry ingredients. Beat at medium speed 2 minutes longer, scraping bowl frequently. Stir in apple, dates and lemon peel. Pour into prepared pan.

Bake at 350°F, 1 hour to 1 hour 15 minutes, or until wooden pick inserted in center comes out clean. Let stand 10 minutes. Invert onto serving plate. Cool slightly. Sift confectioners sugar onto cake. Serve warm. Top with *whipped cream*, if desired.

1 ring cake

Pictured on pages 102-103.

Chocolate Zucchini Cupcakes

1½ cups unsifted all-purpose flour
¾ cup sugar
¼ cup cocoa
1½ teaspoons baking soda
½ teaspoon salt
1 cup shredded, peeled zucchini
⅓ cup Crisco Oil
⅓ cup buttermilk
1 egg
1 teaspoon vanilla

Frosting:
1½ cups confectioners sugar
2 tablespoons butter or margarine, softened
2 to 3 tablespoons milk, divided
¼ teaspoon vanilla

Preheat oven to 350°F. Place paper liners in 12 muffin cups. Set aside.

Mix flour, sugar, cocoa, baking soda and salt in medium mixing bowl. Add remaining cake ingredients. Beat at low speed of electric mixer until ingredients are moistened, scraping bowl constantly. Beat at high speed 1 minute, scraping bowl occasionally. Pour into lined muffin cups, filling each about ⅔ full. Bake at 350°F, 20 to 25 minutes, or until wooden pick inserted in center comes out clean. Remove from pan. Cool completely on wire rack.

For frosting, combine confectioners sugar, butter, 1 tablespoon milk and vanilla in small mixing bowl. Beat at low speed of electric mixer until smooth, scraping bowl frequently. Beat in additional milk to make desired consistency. Spread on cooled cupcakes.

1 dozen cupcakes

Orange Pumpkin Bars

1½ cups unsifted all-purpose flour
1 teaspoon baking powder
1 teaspoon pumpkin pie spice
½ teaspoon baking soda
½ teaspoon salt
1 cup canned pumpkin
¾ cup granulated sugar
⅔ cup Crisco Oil
2 eggs
¼ cup packed light brown sugar
2 tablespoons orange juice
½ cup chopped nuts
½ cup raisins

Icing:
1½ cups confectioners sugar
2 tablespoons orange juice
2 tablespoons butter or margarine, softened
½ teaspoon grated orange peel

Preheat oven to 350°F. Grease and flour 12×8-inch baking dish. Set aside.

Mix flour, baking powder, pumpkin pie spice, baking soda and salt in medium mixing bowl. Set aside. Combine pumpkin, granulated sugar, Crisco Oil, eggs, brown sugar and orange juice in large mixing bowl. Beat at low speed of electric mixer until blended, scraping bowl constantly. Add flour mixture. Beat at medium speed until smooth, scraping bowl frequently. Stir in nuts and raisins. Pour into prepared pan. Bake at 350°F, about 35 minutes, or until center springs back when touched lightly. Cool completely.

For icing, combine all ingredients. Beat at medium speed of electric mixer until smooth. Spread onto cooled cake.

24 bars

Pineapple Orange Chiffon Cake ▼

3 eggs, separated
1½ cups sugar, divided
2 cups unsifted all-purpose flour
1 tablespoon baking powder
1 teaspoon salt
1 can (6 ounces) unsweetened
  pineapple juice
⅓ cup Crisco Oil
¼ cup milk
2 teaspoons grated orange peel

Filling:
⅔ cup pineapple preserves
⅓ cup orange marmalade

Frosting:
1 cup whipping cream
½ teaspoon grated orange peel
¼ cup confectioners sugar

Preheat oven to 350°F. Grease and flour two 9-inch round pans. Set aside.

Place egg whites in medium mixing bowl. Beat at high speed of electric mixer until foamy. Add ½ cup sugar, 1 tablespoon at a time, while beating at high speed until stiff peaks form. Set aside.

Mix remaining 1 cup sugar, flour, baking powder and salt in large mixing bowl. Add pineapple juice, Crisco Oil, milk, orange peel and egg yolks. Beat at low speed of electric mixer until ingredients are moistened, scraping bowl constantly. Beat at high speed 2 minutes, scraping bowl occasionally. Fold in egg white mixture. Pour into prepared pans. Bake at 350°F, 30 to 35 minutes, or until wooden pick inserted in center comes out clean. Cool 10 minutes. Remove from pans. Cool completely on wire rack.

For filling, mix pineapple preserves and orange marmalade in small mixing bowl. Spread some of mixture on top of one layer. Top with remaining layer. Spread top with remaining mixture.

For frosting, place whipping cream in chilled medium mixing bowl. Beat at high speed of electric mixer until thickened. Add orange peel. Gradually add confectioners sugar while beating at high speed until stiff peaks form. Spread on sides and top of cake. Serve immediately or refrigerate. Garnish with *orange slices* or *orange zest*, if desired.

One 2-layer cake

Honey Orange Crescent Cookies ▶

3¼ cups unsifted all-purpose flour
1 teaspoon ground cinnamon
¾ teaspoon baking powder
¾ teaspoon baking soda
¼ teaspoon ground cloves
¼ teaspoon ground nutmeg
¼ teaspoon salt
1½ cups Crisco Oil
7 tablespoons frozen orange juice concentrate, thawed, divided
⅓ cup sugar
1½ teaspoons grated orange peel
1¼ cups very finely-chopped pecans, divided
¼ cup honey

Mix flour, cinnamon, baking powder, baking soda, cloves, nutmeg and salt in medium mixing bowl. Set aside. Mix Crisco Oil, 6 tablespoons orange juice concentrate, sugar and orange peel in large mixing bowl. Blend in flour mixture. Stir in ¾ cup pecans. Cover and refrigerate 2 hours.

Preheat oven to 350°F. Shape chilled dough by scant tablespoonfuls into crescents, each 2½ to 3 inches long. Place about 2 inches apart on ungreased baking sheet. Flatten with fingers to ½-inch thickness.

Bake at 350°F, 12 to 16 minutes, or until edges are light brown. Arrange close together on wire rack over waxed paper. Cool.

Blend honey and remaining 1 tablespoon orange juice concentrate in small bowl. Drizzle over cooled cookies. Sprinkle with remaining ½ cup pecans.

3 to 3½ dozen cookies

◀ Granola Cookies

1 cup sugar
½ cup Crisco Oil
⅓ cup honey
2 eggs
¼ cup water
2 cups unsifted all-purpose flour
1¾ cups quick-cooking rolled oats
1 teaspoon baking soda
1 teaspoon salt
1 teaspoon ground cinnamon
½ cup chopped dried apricots
½ cup raisins
½ cup chopped nuts
½ cup miniature semisweet chocolate chips
½ cup flaked coconut

Preheat oven to 350°F. Grease baking sheet. Set aside.

Mix sugar, Criso Oil, honey, eggs and water in large mixing bowl. Add flour, oats, baking soda, salt and cinnamon. Mix well. Stir in remaining ingredients.

Drop by teaspoonfuls about 2 inches apart onto prepared baking sheet. Bake at 350°F, about 8 minutes, or until almost no indentation remains when touched lightly. Cool on wire rack.

Granola Bars: Follow recipe above, except spread dough in greased and floured 15 × 10-inch jelly roll pan. Bake at 350°F, about 15 minutes, or until top is light brown. Cool completely. Cut into 48 bars.

4½ to 5 dozen cookies or 48 bars

◀ Date-Filled Cookies

3½ cups unsifted all-purpose flour
1 teaspoon baking powder
½ teaspoon baking soda
½ teaspoon salt
1 cup sugar
⅓ cup Crisco Oil
3 eggs
1 tablespoon lemon juice
1 teaspoon grated lemon peel
1 teaspoon vanilla

Filling:
1 package (8 ounces) pitted dates, cut up
¼ cup water
2 tablespoons lemon juice
Dash ground cinnamon

Mix flour, baking powder, baking soda and salt in medium mixing bowl. Set aside. Combine sugar, Crisco Oil, eggs, lemon juice, lemon peel and vanilla in large mixing bowl. Mix well. Stir in flour mixture. Cover and refrigerate at least 2 hours.

Meanwhile, for filling, combine all ingredients in small saucepan. Cook over moderate heat, stirring constantly, until thick. Set aside to cool. Lightly grease baking sheet. Set aside.

Preheat oven to 350°F. Place dough on lightly-floured surface. Divide dough in half. Roll each half to ⅛-inch thickness. Cut into 3-inch rounds. Place 1 teaspoon date mixture on center of each round. Fold in half over date mixture. Press edges lightly to seal. Place on prepared baking sheet. Bake at 350°F, 10 to 12 minutes, or until light brown. Cool on wire rack.

3 dozen cookies

Lemon Tea Cookies ▼

3¼ cups unsifted all-purpose flour
1½ teaspoons baking powder
¼ teaspoon salt
¾ cup butter or margarine, softened
¾ cup granulated sugar
¾ cup confectioners sugar
½ cup Crisco Oil
2 eggs
2 teaspoons grated lemon peel
2 teaspoons lemon extract
  Granulated sugar

Mix flour, baking powder and salt in small mixing bowl. Set aside. Cream butter, granulated sugar and confectioners sugar in large mixing bowl. Blend in Crisco Oil, eggs, lemon peel and lemon extract. Stir in flour mixture. Cover and refrigerate about 2 hours.

Preheat oven to 350°F. Shape dough into 1-inch balls. Place 2 to 3 inches apart on ungreased baking sheet. Flatten to ⅛-inch thickness with bottom of drinking glass dipped in granulated sugar. Bake at 350°F, 10 to 12 minutes, or until edges are light golden brown. Remove cookies from pan immediately. Cool on wire rack.

Lemon Crisps: Follow recipe above, except shape dough into ¾-inch balls and flatten to ¹⁄₁₆-inch thickness with sugar-dipped glass. Bake 7 to 9 minutes, or until edges are light golden brown.

6 to 7 dozen cookies

Chocolate Crackles ▼

1½ cups granulated sugar
½ cup Crisco Oil
1½ teaspoons vanilla
3 eggs
1⅔ cups unsifted all-purpose flour
½ cup cocoa
1½ teaspoons baking powder
½ teaspoon salt
⅓ to ½ cup confectioners sugar

Combine granulated sugar, Crisco Oil and vanilla in medium mixing bowl. Mix well. Add eggs, one at a time, mixing well after each addition. Stir in flour, cocoa, baking powder and salt. Cover and refrigerate about 3 hours.

Preheat oven to 350°F. Lightly grease baking sheet. Set aside. Place confectioners sugar in shallow dish or large plastic food storage bag. Shape dough into 1-inch balls. Roll in confectioners sugar or add to bag and shake to coat. Place about 2 inches apart on prepared baking sheet. Bake at 350°F, about 10 minutes*, or until almost no indentation remains when touched lightly. Cool on wire rack.

*For softer cookies, bake about 8 minutes.

4 to 5 dozen cookies

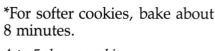

Deep-Fried Sour Cream Cookies

1⅔ cups unsifted all-purpose flour
 1 tablespoon granulated sugar
 ½ teaspoon salt
 ½ cup dairy sour cream
 3 egg yolks, slightly beaten
 2 tablespoons Crisco Oil
 1 teaspoon vanilla
   Crisco Oil for frying
   Confectioners sugar

Mix flour, granulated sugar and salt in medium mixing bowl. Make a well in center of mixture. Set aside. Blend sour cream, egg yolks, Crisco Oil and vanilla in small mixing bowl. Pour into well in dry ingredients. Mix with fork. Transfer mixture to lightly-floured surface. Knead until blended. Roll dough to ⅛-inch thickness. Cut into diamond shapes, 3 inches long and 2 inches wide.

Heat 2 to 3 inches Crisco Oil in deep-fryer or large saucepan to 375°F. Fry a few cookies at a time, about 1½ minutes, or until light golden brown, turning over once. Drain on paper towels. Sprinkle with confectioners sugar or cinnamon-sugar.

About 2 dozen cookies

Rosettes

   Crisco Oil for frying
 1 cup unsifted all-purpose flour
 2 tablespoons confectioners sugar
 ¼ teaspoon salt
 1 cup milk
 2 eggs
 1 teaspoon vanilla
 1 teaspoon almond extract
   Confectioners sugar

Heat 2 to 3 inches Crisco Oil in deep-fryer or large saucepan to 365°F. Meanwhile, mix flour, 2 tablespoons confectioners sugar and salt in small mixing bowl. Add milk, eggs, vanilla and almond extract. Stir until smooth.

Place rosette iron in hot Crisco Oil 1 minute. Tap excess oil from iron onto paper towel. Dip hot iron into batter, making sure batter does not cover top of iron. Place back into hot oil. Fry about 30 seconds, or until rosette is golden brown. Immediately remove rosette. Drain on paper towels. Reheat iron in hot oil 1 minute before frying each rosette. Sprinkle rosettes with confectioners sugar.

3 dozen rosettes

How to Make Rosettes

Dip hot iron into batter. Be sure batter does not cover top of iron.

Index